DISCOVERING AMERICA

Western Great Lakes

ILLINOIS • IOWA • MINNESOTA • WISCONSIN

By
Thomas G. Aylesworth
Virginia L. Aylesworth

CHELSEA HOUSE PUBLISHERS
New York • Philadelphia

First Printing

1   3   5   7   9   8   6   4   2

Library of Congress Cataloging-in-Publication Data

Aylesworth, Thomas G.
     Western Great Lakes: Illinois, Iowa, Minnesota, Wisconsin
Thomas G. Aylesworth, Virginia L. Aylesworth.
       p. cm.—(Discovering America)
       Includes bibliographical references and index.
       ISBN 0-7910-3242-6.
          0-7910-3423-2 (pbk.)
       1. Lake States—Juvenile literature. 2. Illinois—Juvenile literature. 3. Iowa—Juvenile literature.
4. Minnesota—Juvenile literature. 5. Wisconsin—Juvenile literature. I. Aylesworth, Virginia
L. II. Title. III. Series: Aylesworth, Thomas G. Discovering America.

F551.A955   1995   94-40425
977—dc20   CIP
                                                          AC

CONTENTS

Illinois

The state seal of Illinois, designed by the secretary of state Sharon Tyndale, was first used in 1868. The current seal is the third in Illinois history. In the center of the circular seal is an American eagle holding a shield with stars and stripes representing the 13 original states. In the eagle's beak is a scroll bearing the state motto. Under the shield is an olive branch, symbolizing peace, and nearby is a boulder with two dates, 1818 (the year Illinois entered the Union) and 1868 (the year the seal was adopted). Around the top of the circle is inscribed "Seal of the State of Illinois," and at the bottom is the date August 26th, 1818—the date the first state constitution was adopted.

WISCONSIN

■ GALENA

Waukegan ●

Freeport ●

Rockford ●

Elgin

IOWA

De Kalb ● Wheaton ● **Chicago**

LISLE ■ ■ BROOKFIELD

Aurora ●

Joliet ●

East Moline ●

Rock Island

Kankakee ●

Galesburg ●

INDIANA

■ NAUVOO
RESTORATION

Peoria ●

Pekin ● ● Normal

Bloomington ●

Rantoul ●

Quincy ●

Champaign ● Danville ●

Urbana ●

Springfield

● Decatur

Jacksonville ●

★

■
LINCOLN HOME
NATIONAL HISTORICAL SITE

Mississippi River

Alton ●

Granite City ●

● Belleville

ILLINOIS

Wabash River

N
△

MISSOURI

Ohio River

KENTUCKY

★ State Capital
● Cities or towns
■ OF SPECIAL INTEREST

10 20   40   60   80   100   120   Miles
10 20   40   60   80   100   120   140   160   180   200 Kilometres

Capital: Springfield

State Flower:
Wood Violet

ILLINOIS
At a Glance

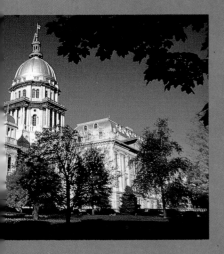

State Flag

Major Industries: Manufacturing, mining, agriculture, livestock

State Bird: Cardinal

Size: 56,345 square miles (24th largest)
Population: 11,631,131 (6th largest)

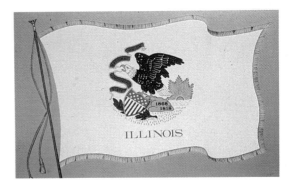

State Flag

The Illinois state flag, adopted in 1915, bears a modification of the state seal set on a white background.

State Motto

State Sovereignty, National Union

Inscribed on the state seal, first adopted in 1818, this motto reflects the idea that the state rules itself, but is subservient to the nation.

Canoeing on Devils Kitchen Lake.

State Capital

The first capital was at Kaskaskia (1818-20). It was then moved to Vandalia (1820-39), and finally in 1839, to Springfield.

State Name and Nicknames

Illinois was named by the French explorer Robert Cavelier, Sieur de La Salle, in 1679. It was the French spelling of the Indian word *illini*, which means warrior or member of the Illinois tribe.

The most common nickname for Illinois is the *Prairie State* because of the vast prairies in the territory. It is also called the *Corn State* because of the importance of that crop to the farmers of the region. Illinois has an official state slogan, adopted in 1955—"The Land of Lincoln"—since it was here that the Great Emancipator began his political career.

State Flower

In 1907, Illinois schoolchildren voted for the state flower from a list. The violet, *Viola pedatifida*, won and it was decreed the state flower in 1908.

State Tree

The children also voted in 1907 for a state tree, and the native oak was selected in 1908. But there are two oak trees native to the state, the northern red oak and the white oak, so the children voted a second time. The white oak, *Quercus alba*, was adopted in 1973.

State Bird

Schoolchildren chose the cardinal, *Cardinalis cardinalis*, as state bird in 1929.

State Animal

The white-tailed deer, *Odocoileus virginianus*, was named the state animal in 1982.

State Insect

The monarch butterfly, *Danaus plexippus*, was adopted as state insect in 1975.

State Language

English has been the state language of Illinois since 1969.

State Mineral

Fluorite was named state mineral in 1965.

State Song

In 1925, "Illinois," words by Charles H. Chamberlain and music by Archibald Johnston, was made the state song.

Population

The population of Illinois in 1992 was 11,631,131, making it the 6th most populous state. There are 209.2 persons per square mile.

Industries

The principal industries of Illinois are trade, finance, insurance, foods, and agriculture. The chief manufactured products are machinery, electric and electronic equipment, metals, chemicals, printing, and publishing.

Agriculture

The chief crops of the state are corn, soybeans, wheat, oats, and hay. Illinois is also a livestock state, and there are estimated to be some 1.98 million cattle, 5.9 million hogs and pigs, 129,000 sheep, and 3.31 million chickens and turkeys on its farms. Oak, hickory, maple, and cottonwood trees are harvested. Crushed stone, cement, sand, and gravel are important mineral resources. Commercial fishing earned $367,000 in 1992.

Government

The governor of Illinois is elected to a four-year term, as are the lieutenant governor, attorney general, secretary of state, comptroller, and treasurer. The state legislature, called the general assembly, which meets annually, consists of a senate of 59 members and a house of representatives of 118 members. The senators are elected to four-year terms and the representatives to two-year terms. The most recent state constitution was adopted in 1970. In addition to its two U.S. senators, Illinois has 20 representatives in the U.S. House of Representatives. The state has 24 votes in the electoral college.

Sports

Illinois is a sport-conscious state and always has been. In 1896 in Chicago, the University of Chicago beat the University of Iowa in the first basketball game using five men on each side. In 1901 the first American Bowling Congress National Championship Tournament was held in Chicago. On the collegiate level, the NCAA national basketball championship was won by Loyola University of Chicago in 1963, and the National Invitation Tournament, by Bradley University (1957, 1960, 1964, 1982), De Paul University (1945), and Southern Illinois University (1967). In football, the Rose Bowl has been won by the University of Illinois (1947, 1952, 1964) and Northwestern University (1949).

On the professional level, Chicago is home to several teams. The Cubs of the National League play baseball at Wrigley Field, and the White Sox of the American League play in Comiskey Park. The Bears of the National Football League hold their games in Soldier Field, and the Bulls of the National Basketball Association and Blackhawks of the National Hockey League share Chicago Stadium.

An afternoon of sailing on Lake Michigan, which borders Illinois.

Major Cities

Chicago (population 2,783,726). Settled in 1803, the territory was mapped in 1673 by Louis Jolliet, and the first trading post was established in 1796. The city didn't start its real growth as an industrial and cultural center until the mid-1800s. The name came from the Indian word *Checagou*, which seems to have several meanings. Chicago is a city of beautiful parks, monumental architecture, and dynamic people.

Things to see in Chicago: Chicago Public Library Cultural Center, Monadnock Building (1889-93), Rookery (1886), Chicago Board of Trade (1929), Sears Tower, Chicago Mercantile Exchange, Navy Pier, John Hancock Center, Water Tower (1969), Chicago *Tribune* Tower, Wrigley Building, Newberry Library (1887), Robie House, Jane Addams' Hull House (1856), Art Institute of Chicago, Museum of Contemporary Art, Terra Museum of American Art, Peace Museum, Chicago Historical

A prehistoric creature is displayed at the Field Museum of Natural History, in the Grant Park area of Chicago.

Society, Chicago Academy of Sciences, Adler Planetarium, John G. Shedd Aquarium, Field Museum of Natural History, Chicago Fire Academy, Museum of Science and Industry, Oriental Institute Museum, Morton B. Weiss Museum of Judaica, Du Sable Museum of African-American History, Chicago Temple, Moody Church, Our

Lady of Sorrows Basilica, Lincoln Park Zoological Gardens, Lincoln Park Conservatory, and the Garfield Park Conservatory.

Rockford (population 139,943). Founded in 1834, the second-largest city in the state is located on the Rock River. The first settlers were from New England, but today much of the population is of Swedish and Italian descent. Rockford is an important industrial city.

Things to see in Rockford: Tinker Swiss Cottage (1865), Time Museum, Midway Village/Rockford Museum Center, Burpee Museum of Natural History, Rockford Art Museum, Zitelman Scout Museum, John Erlander Home (1871), Sinnissippi Park, Rockford Trolley, and *Forest City Queen.*

Springfield (population 105,227). Settled in 1819, the capital city of Illinois was laid out near the geographical center of the state. The city is most famous as the home of Abraham Lincoln for the 25 years before he was elected president.

Things to see in Springfield:
State Capitol, Illinois State Museum, Old State Capitol State Historic Site, Lincoln's Tomb State Historic Site, Lincoln Home National Historic Site, Oliver P. Parks Telephone Museum, Dana-Thomas House State Historic Site (1902-04), Lincoln Depot, Lincoln-Herndon Building, Vachel Lindsay Home (1846), Thomas Rees Memorial Carillon, Lincoln Memorial Garden and Nature Center, Executive Mansion, Edwards Place (1833), and Henson Robinson Zoo.

Abraham Lincoln's Springfield home of sixteen years is now the Lincoln Home National Historic Site. Three of his sons were born there.

Places to Visit

The National Park Service maintains two areas in the state of Illinois: Lincoln Home National Historic Site and Shawnee National Forest. In addition, there are 73 state recreation areas.

Antioch: Hiram Butrick Sawmill. This is a working replica of an 1839 waterpowered sawmill that was the center of the town.

Brookfield: Brookfield Zoo. One of the world's finest zoos features indoor rain forests and dolphin shows.

Cahokia: Cahokia Courthouse State Historic Site. A restoration of the oldest house in the state, which was built around 1737.

Charleston: Lincoln Log Cabin State Historic Site. The Thomas Lincoln Log Cabin, where the family lived after 1837, has been reconstructed here.

East St. Louis: Katherine Dunham Museum. A collection of African and Caribbean artifacts collected by the dancer and choreographer is exhibited.

Elgin: Fox River Trolley Museum. Early trolleys and railway equipment can be seen and rides can be taken

on early 1900s cars.

Galena: Ulysses S. Grant Home State Historic Site. This house was given to Grant by his native city after the Civil War.

Galesburg: Carl Sandburg State Historical Site. Built in 1874, this was the home of the famous poet and historian.

Glenview: Hartung's Automotive Museum. More than 100 antique autos and trucks are displayed here.

Havana: Dickson Mounds State Museum. Remains of prehistoric Indian life can be seen here.

Highwood: Fort Sheridan. The fort was founded in 1887 and contains 94 old buildings and exhibits of military history.

La Grange: Historic District. Buildings dating from the late nineteenth and early twentieth centuries, including some designed by Frank Lloyd Wright, can be seen.

Lisle: Morton Arboretum. This bucolic area of about 1,500 acres contains some 5,000 kinds of trees and other plants.

Macomb: Clarence Watson/ Wiley Schoolhouse Museum. This restored 1877 one-room schoolhouse still contains many of the original fixtures.

Naperville: Naper Settlement. This 12-acre outdoor history museum with 25 buildings recreates a northern Illinois town of the nineteenth century.

Nauvoo: Nauvoo Restoration. Nauvoo was founded as a Mormon community. The Brigham Young Home and many other structures here are open to the public.

Oak Brook: Old Graue Mill and Museum. This restored 1852 mill is the only operating waterpowered gristmill in the state.

Oak Park: Frank Lloyd Wright Home and Studio. Several buildings designed by the architect, including his own home and studio, and the Unity Temple, can be seen here.

Oregon: Stronghold Castle. This authentic old English castle was built in the early part of the century.

Petersburg: Lincoln's New Salem State Historic Site. This is a reconstruction of the town of New Salem when Lincoln lived there.

Princeton: Owen Lovejoy Homestead. Built in 1838, this was the home of the abolitionist preacher as well as a stop on the Underground Railroad.

Rock Island: Black Hawk State Historic Site. This is the site of the western-most battle of the Revolutionary War.

Salem: William Jennings Bryan Birthplace/Museum. The restored birthplace of the famous orator was built in 1852.

Union: Illinois Railway Museum. Historic and antique railroad cars, engines, and coaches are displayed on the museum's 56 acres.

Vandalia: Vandalia Statehouse State Historic Site. This was built in 1836, when the town was the state capital.

Woodstock: Woodstock Opera House. This restored "Steamboat Gothic" theater dates back to 1889.

Events

There are many events and organizations that schedule activities of various kinds in the state of Illinois. Here are some of them.

Sports: Chicago to Mackinac Races (Chicago), Mid-America Canoe Race (Elgin), Elgin National Road Race (Elgin), Santa Fe Speedway (Hinsdale), Kankakee River Valley Bicycle Classic (Kankakee), Kankakee River Valley Regatta (Kankakee), Western Open Golf Tournament (Oak Brook), Polo (Oak Brook), Montreal Canoe Weekends (Peru), Grand Prix of Karting (Quincy), Rockford Speedway

A beautiful afternoon for baseball at Wrigley Field, home of the Chicago Cubs.

(Rockford), LPGA Rail Charity Golf Classic (Springfield).

Arts and Crafts: Sommarmarknad (Bishop Hill), Ewing Arts Festival (Bloomington), Chicago International Art Exposition (Chicago), Gold Coast Art Fair (Chicago), Fountain Square Arts Festival (Evanston), Lakefront Art Fair (Evanston), Gladiolus Festival (Kankakee), Greenwich Village Art Fair (Rockford), Clayville Folk Crafts Festival (Springfield).

Music: Hubbard Street Dance Company (Chicago), Mordine and Company (Chicago), Chicago Opera Theater (Chicago), Lyric Opera of Chicago (Chicago), Chicago Symphony (Chicago), Chicago Civic Orchestra (Chicago), Grant Park Symphony (Chicago), Civic Opera (Chicago), Jazz Festival (Chicago), Band Concerts (Elgin), Rootabaga Jazz Festival (Galesburg), Ravinia Festival (Highland Park), International Carillon Festival (Springfield), Municipal Band Concerts (Springfield), Springfield Muni Opera (Springfield).

Entertainment: Bishop Hill Jordbruksdagarna (Bishop Hill), Harvest Frolic (Charleston), St. Patrick's Day Parade (Chicago), Taste of Chicago (Chicago), Air and Water Show (Chicago), Electric Railroad Fair (Elgin),

It's maple syrup time in the woods of Lincoln Memorial Garden in Springfield.

Custer's Last Stand (Evanston), Antique Town Rod Run (Galena), Geneva Swedish Festival (Geneva), Pet Parade (La Grange), Old Canal Days (Lockport), Joe Naper Day (Naperville), Steamboat Days (Peoria), Winter Wilderness Weekend (Peru), National Sweet Corn Festival (Peru), Burgoo Festival (Peru), Calftown Strassenfest (Quincy), Winter Carnival (Rockford), Mid-America Horse Festival (St. Charles), Maple Syrup Time (Springfield), Illinois State Fair (Springfield).

Tours: Loop Walking Tour (Chicago), June Open House (Galena), Fall Tour of Homes (Galena), Wildflower Pilgrimage (Peru), Candlelight Tour of New Salem (Petersburg).

Theater: The American Passion Play (Bloomington), Illinois Shakespeare Festival (Bloomington), Arie Crown (Chicago), Body Politic (Chicago), Goodman Theater (Chicago), Second City (Chicago), Stage Coach Theater (De Kalb), Poplar Creek Music Theater (Hoffman Estates), Rialto Square Theatre (Joliet), Bicentennial Park Theater (Joliet), *City of Joseph* (Nauvoo), New American Theater (Rockford), Genesius Guild (Rock Island), Centre East for the Arts (Skokie).

Illinois has been nicknamed the "Prairie State" because much of the region contains large expanses of flat, grassy land.

The Land and the Climate

One of the nicknames of Illinois is the Prairie State, and this is a reasonably accurate description. Much of the land is level, and it was once covered with prairie grass. There are a few areas of low, rolling hills and a few sections of natural forest. The extreme northwest has the highest point in the state, at 1,235 feet, while the lowest point is in the south, at 279 feet, where the Mississippi and Ohio Rivers meet.

Illinois has three main land regions. The Central Plains are part of the fertile Interior Plains that cover most of the Midwest. About 90 percent of the land in Illinois is in these plains, which were leveled by great glaciers during the Ice Age. The Central Plains are further divided into the Great Lakes Plains (from Chicago to the northern border), the Driftless Area (in the extreme northwest), and the Till Plains (covering most of the state). The Till Plains have been called "the Garden Spot of the Nation" because of their rich soil, ideal for grain crops.

Stretching across the southern part of the state for about 70 miles are the Shawnee Hills, which are sometimes called "the Illinois Ozarks." This strip is between five and forty miles wide. It is a region of valleys, hills, river bluffs, and forests.

The Gulf Coastal Plain is located along the extreme southern border of the state. The northern part is hilly, the southern part, flat. The early settlers called this area Egypt because of its resemblance to the Nile Delta. The largest city in this area along the Ohio and Mississippi Rivers is Cairo, the unofficial capital of what is now called Little Egypt.

The fertile river valleys of Southern Illinois provide farm with rich soil, ideal for grain production.

Above:
O'Hare airport, located in Chicago, is the busiest in the country.

Right:
Much of Chicago overlooks Lake Michigan. In the winter, cold temperatures combined with strong winds that blow off the lake, often make for severe conditions.

Illinois has 63 miles of shoreline along Lake Michigan. There are about 500 rivers and streams in the state, of which the most important, besides the Ohio and Mississippi, are the Chicago, Des Plaines, Illinois, and Sangamon Rivers.

With little to break the sweep of the prevailing west-to-east winds, the weather is subject to sharp changes in temperature. Chicago has an average January temperature of about 26 degrees F. and an average of 75 degrees F. in summer. Zero temperatures in winter are not uncommon in the north, and summer temperatures often rise to over 100 degrees F. The annual rainfall is between 30 and 35 inches.

The History

The first people in Illinois, the prehistoric Indians called Mound Builders, had disappeared before the European explorers came, but more than 10,000 of their earthen burial and temple mounds still stand. Later, other regional tribes formed what is called the Illinois Confederacy. The Algonkian tribes in the Confederacy were the Cahokia, Kaskaskia, Michigamea, Moingwena, Peoria, and Tamaroa. Other tribes living in the Great Lakes area included the Fox, Sauk, Chippewa, Illinois, and Winnebago.

French Jesuit missionary Jacques Marquette and French-Canadian explorer Louis Joliet traveled down the Illinois River in 1673 followed by French explorer Robert Cavelier, Sieur de la Salle. The region remained peaceful until the Iroquois Indians attacked the Illinois Indians in 1690. In 1699 French priests founded a mission at Cahokia, a fur-trading post, which was the first permanent town in Illinois. Other missions were established at La Salle, Marseilles, and Champaign.

In 1717 Illinois became part of the French colony of Louisiana, and John Law, a Scottish financial promoter who lived in Paris, organized a company that brought French settlers to Illinois. Three years later these colonists built Fort de Chartres, about 20 miles northwest of Kaskaskia on the east bank of the Mississippi River. In 1763 the British from the East defeated the French in the French and Indian Wars that had been going on intermittently for almost seventy-five years. France gave the Illinois region to England.

Until the end of the Revolutionary War, there were only about 1,000 white people in what would become the state of Illinois. This group included missionaries, fur traders, French and English settlers, and British troops. In 1778 George Rogers Clark of Virginia and a band of frontiersmen called "The Big Knives" captured Kaskaskia and Cahokia from the British soldiers; that area became part of Virginia. New settlers came in from nearby territories, as the frontier kept moving westward.

In 1784 Virginia gave the Illinois region to the U.S. Government. Congress first made the region a part of the Northwest Territory in 1787. Then Illinois became part of the Indiana Territory in 1801. Finally, the Illinois Territory was created from what is now Illinois and Wisconsin, with Kaskaskia as its capital.

During the early 1800s, when there were only about 12,000 people in the future state of Illinois, the Indians became restless because the settlers were taking so much of their land. During the War of 1812, the Indians fought on the side of the British. The bloodiest Indian attack on the Americans took place in August 1812, when the Potawatomi tribe massacred many settlers withdrawing from Fort Dearborn at the mouth of the Chicago River. (This would later be the site of the great city of Chicago.)

On December 3, 1818, Illinois became the 21st state of the Union, although only the southern part of the state was settled. The voters elected Shadrach Bond as their first governor. In 1819 Vandalia was selected as the state capital for a 20-year period (1820–1840).

By 1830 the population of the state had risen to 157,000, partly as a result of the opening of the Erie Canal in New York State, which made it easier to travel to the Midwest. The Federal Government moved many Illinois Indians west of the Mississippi the following year. In the Black Hawk War of 1832, the settlers defeated the Sauk

This engraving shows the city of Chicago in 1849, one year after completion of the Illinois and Michigan Canal. The canal ran between Chicago and La Salle and provided many jobs for the predominantly Irish immigrants in the region at that time.

An engraving done in 1857 of Fort Dearborn, which was located at the mouth of the Chicago River. It was here in 1812 that the Potawatomi Indians surprised American settlers in one of the bloodiest attacks of the war. The fort was completely destroyed by the Indians and later rebuilt by the settlers.

and Fox Indians, who had resisted the seizure of their ancestral lands as long as they could. This eliminated the fear of Indian attacks and many immigrants poured into the state during the mid-1830s. The Irish came to work on the Illinois and Michigan Canal between Chicago and La Salle (completed in 1848). Others came from all over Europe to farm, build railroads, and work in factories and mines. Invention of the steel plow by John Deere, and of the reaping machine by Cyrus H. McCormick of Chicago, made large-scale farming possible in the 1830s and '40s. In 1839 the state capital was moved to Springfield, which was in a more central location than Vandalia now that the northern part of Illinois had been settled.

During the Civil War, despite the fact that the Union President, Abraham Lincoln, was an Illinois lawyer, there were many Southern sympathizers in the state. Some even considered forming a separate state. But the majority was pro-Union: more than a quarter of a million Illinois soldiers served in the Union Army, and the North's greatest general (later president), Ulysses S. Grant, was from Galena.

After the Civil War, Illinois became a vital railroad link between East and West; factories, forges, and mills sprang up by the dozen.

A portrait by G. Healy of Illinois's most famous lawyer, Abraham Lincoln. It was in Illinois in 1858 that Lincoln ran against Stephen Douglas for a seat in the Senate. The most important factors in the election were the Lincoln-Douglas debates, which focused on the subject of slavery. Lincoln argued that slavery was "a moral, a social, and a political wrong." Douglas said that the question was a personal one, which should be decided by the individual. Although Douglas won the Senatorial election, Lincoln won his later campaign for the Presidency in 1860. It was during his term in the White House that Lincoln issued the Emancipation Proclamation, which abolished slavery in 1863.

Fast-growing Chicago became the nation's grain and meat-packing center—until the Great Fire of 1871 destroyed much of the city. Four square miles of the city, including the business district, were destroyed; 250 people died; over 90,000 people were left homeless; and approximately $200 million in damages were caused. Chicago was rebuilt in record time. Only twelve years later, Chicago opened its first World's Fair—the Columbian Exposition, featuring the world's first Ferris wheel.

By 1900 more than half the people of Illinois lived in cities, although agriculture remained an important part of the economy. The state had become one of the most progressive in the Union, passing child labor laws, limiting the work week for women, and setting up a state welfare system. Sometimes the price of reform was high. In 1886 at least 10 people were killed in Chicago's Haymarket Square Riot, when discontented laborers clashed with police.

Between 1890 and 1920, Chicago experienced a cultural Renaissance. Popular writers including Eugene Field, Peter Finley Dunne, Hamlin Garland, Henry Blake Fuller, Theodore Dreiser and Carl Sandburg, among others, made Chicago their home. The literary journal *Poetry: A Magazine of Verse* was established at this time. This renaissance was not limited to the emergence of successful writers. Chicago is known as a center of architectural innovation and houses buildings designed by Dankmar Adler, Louis Sullivan, Frank Lloyd Wright, and Henry H. Richardson.

During World War I, Illinois furnished men for an entire army division—the 33rd, or Prairie, Division. Navy men, some 100,000 of them, were trained at the Great Lakes Naval Training Center, and 5,000 army officers were turned out at Fort Sheridan.

In the 1920s, during the era of Prohibition, Chicago developed a reputation for its gangsters and Carl Sandburg nicknamed it "the City of the Big Shoulders." Infamous crime boss Capone eliminated all of his enemies and is remembered for the St. Valentines Day Massacre of

A portrait by G. De Forest of Jane Addams, social reformer and founder of Hull House in 1889. Hull House provided Chicago's immigrant families with various community services in an effort to help them succeed in the unfamiliar, and often unfriendly, cities.

A drawing of Ernest Hemingway, the Illinois-born novelist who spent much of his life in Europe. *The Sun Also Rises,* *A Farewell to Arms,* and *For Whom the Bell Tolls* are among his greatest and most influential works.

1929, when seven henchmen of his rival George "Bugs" Moran were murdered.

In 1933 and 1934 Chicago had its second World's Fair—The Century of Progress Exposition—and the Illinois Waterway, a series of canals and rivers, was opened to traffic from Lake Michigan to the Mississippi. Oil discoveries in Southeastern Illinois (from 1937) helped pull the state out of the Depression.

The era of atomic energy was born in Illinois in 1942, when the first controlled atomic chain reaction was set off by Enrico Fermi and his scientific team at the University of Chicago. During World War II, the state's thousands of war plants contributed to the victory. During the Korean War (1950–1953), more than half of the Illinois National Guard went into active duty. The 1968 Democratic National Convention was held in Chicago and violent clashes between police and anti-war protesters were televised to the entire nation.

In only a century and a half, Illinois has evolved from a frontier wilderness into a vast empire of cities, farms, mines, and mills. Abundant natural resources, notably fertile soil, coal, oil, and other minerals, and valuable forest products, make Illinois a leader in both agriculture and manufacturing.

Education

The Free School System in Illinois began in 1825. Following World War II, schools were consolidated and 12,000 schools in 1944 were reduced to 1,340 schools by 1969. There are 34 locally controlled junior colleges with vocational programs in Illinois. The main public college is the University of Illinois at Urbana. There is also a concentration of medical schools in Illinois—one out of every five U.S. doctors received their medical training in Chicago.

The People

More than 80 percent of the people of Illinois live in cities and towns, over 60 percent of them in the Chicago Metropolitan Area. About seven percent of Illinois residents were born outside the United States, with Germans and Poles being the most numerous ethnic groups. Others were born in Czechoslovakia, Greece, Ireland, Italy, Lithuania, Russia, and Sweden: most of them live in the Chicago area. A third of the church members in the state are Roman Catholic.

Famous People

Many famous people were born in the state of Illinois. Here are a few:

Jane Addams 1860-1935, Cedarville. Co-founder of Hull House

Mary Astor 1906-87, Quincy. Academy Award-winning actress: *The Great Lie, The Maltese Falcon*

John Belushi 1949-1982, Chicago. Television and film actor: *Animal House, Neighbors*

Jack Benny 1894-1974, Chicago. Film, television and radio comedian: *To Be or Not To Be*

Harry Blackmun b. 1908, Nashville. Supreme Court justice

Lou Boudreau b. 1917, Harvey. Hall of Fame baseball player

Ray Bradbury b. 1920,

Waukegan. Novelist: *Fahrenheit 451*

William Jennings Bryan 1860-1925, Salem. Orator and presidential candidate

Edgar Rice Burroughs 1875-1950, Chicago. Novelist: *Tarzan* books

Dick Butkus b. 1942, Chicago. Hall of Fame football player

Raymond Chandler 1888-1959, Chicago. Novelist: *Farewell, My Lovely*

Hillary Rodham Clinton b. 1947, Chicago. Lawyer and First Lady of the United States

Jimmy Connors b. 1952, Belleville. Tennis champion

Miles Davis 1926-91, Alton. Jazz trumpeter

Walt Disney 1901-66, Chicago. Animation producer

John Dos Passos 1896-1970, Chicago. Novelist: *Manhattan Transfer, U.S.A.*

Wyatt Earp 1848-1929, Monmouth. Western law officer

James T. Farrell 1904-79, Chicago. Novelist: *The Young Manhood of Studs Lonigan*

Bobby Fischer b. 1943, Chicago. Champion chess player

Harrison Ford b. 1942, Chicago. Film actor: *Star Wars, Raiders of the Lost Ark*

Bob Fosse 1927-87, Chicago. Stage and film director

Betty Friedan b. 1921, Peoria. Feminist

Arthur Goldberg 1908-90, Chicago. Supreme Court Justice

Benny Goodman 1909-86, Chicago. Swing clarinetist

Lorraine Hansberry 1930-65, Chicago. Playwright: *A Raisin in the Sun*

Hugh Hefner b. 1926, Chicago. Magazine publisher

Ernest Hemingway 1899-1961, Oak Park. Nobel Prize-winning novelist: *For Whom the Bell Tolls, The Old Man and the Sea*

Charlton Heston b. 1923, Evanston. Academy Award-winning actor: *Ben Hur, Soylent Green*

Wild Bill Hickock 1837-1876, Troy Grove. Western marshal

Rock Hudson 1925-1985, Winnetka. Film actor: *Giant, Pillow Talk*

Burl Ives b. 1909, Hunt Township. Academy Award-winning actor: *Cat on a Hot Tin Roof*

James Jones 1921-77, Robinson. Novelist: *From Here to Eternity*

Quincy Jones b. 1933, Chicago. Composer and arranger

Gene Krupa 1909-73, Chicago. Jazz drummer

Vachel Lindsay 1879-1931, Springfield. Poet: *The Congo and Other Poems*

Archibald MacLeish 1892-1982, Glencoe. Pulitzer Prize-winning poet: *Conquistador*

Jimmy McPartland b. 1907, Chicago. Jazz cornetist

George Mikan b. 1924, Joliet. Hall of Fame basketball player

Sherrill Milnes b. 1935, Downers Grove. Operatic baritone

Vincente Minnelli 1910-86, Chicago. Film director

Bob Newhart b. 1929, Oak Park. Television actor and comedian: *The Bob Newhart Show, Newhart*

Ken Norton b. 1945, Jacksonville. Heavyweight boxing champion

William S. Paley 1901-1990, Chicago. Founder of CBS

Richard Pryor b. 1940, Peoria. Stage and film comedian: *Silver Streak, Stir Crazy*

Edward M. Purcell b. 1912, Taylorville. Nobel Prize-winning physicist

Ronald Reagan b. 1911, Tampico. Fortieth President of the United States

Jason Robards, Jr. b. 1922, Chicago. Academy Award-winning actor: *All the President's Men, Julia*

Carl Sandburg 1878-1967, Galesburg. Pulitzer Prize-winning poet and

Wild Bill Hickock was a marshal and hero of the Old West.

historian: *Complete Poems*

E. W. Scripps 1854-1926, Rushville. Founder of United Press

John Paul Stevens b. 1920, Chicago. Supreme Court justice

Peter Ueberroth b. 1937, Chicago. Baseball commissioner

Carl Van Doren 1885-1950, Hope. Pulitzer Prize-winning biographer

Mark Van Doren 1894-1972, Hope. Pulitzer Prize-winning poet

James D. Watson b. 1928, Chicago. Nobel Prize-winning biochemist

P. K. Wrigley 1894-1977, Chicago. Chewing gum executive

Florenz Ziegfeld 1869-1932, Chicago. Broadway producer

Colleges and Universities

There are many colleges and universities in Illinois. Here are the more prominent, with their locations, dates of founding, and enrollments:

Augustana College, Rock Island, 1860, 2,080

Aurora University, Aurora, 1893, 2,025

Bradley University, Peoria, 1897, 6,191

Chicago State University, Chicago, 1867, 8,675

College of St. Francis, Joliet, 1920, 1,888

Concordia University, River Forest, 1864, 1,726

De Paul University, Chicago, 1898, 16,499

Eastern Illinois University, Charleston, 1895, 11,411

Elmhurst College, Elmhurst, 1871, 2,725

Illinois Benedictine College, Lisle, 1887, 2,982

Illinois College, Jacksonville, 1829, 926

Illinois Institute of Technology, Chicago, 1890, 6,693

Illinois State University, Normal, 1857, 21,765

Illinois Wesleyan University, Bloomington, 1850, 1,822

Knox College, Galesburg, 1837, 954

Lake Forest College, Lake Forest, 1857, 960

Lewis University, Romeoville, 1932, 4,102

Loyola University of Chicago, Chicago, 1870, 15,298

Millikin University, Decatur, 1901, 1,892

North Central College, Naperville, 1861, 2,535

Northern Illinois University, De Kalb, 1895, 24,052

Northwestern University, Evanston, 1851, 12,032

Olivet Nazarene University, Kankakee, 1907, 1,996

Quincy University, Quincy, 1860, 1,223

Rockford College, Rockford, 1847, 1,491

Roosevelt University, Chicago, 1945, 6,444

Rosary College, River Forest, 1901, 1,766

Rush University, Chicago, 1969, 1,301

Saint Xavier University, Chicago, 1847, 3,850

Southern Illinois University at Carbondale, Carbondale, 1869, 24,766; *at Edwardsville,* Edwardsville, 1957, 11,670

University of Chicago, Chicago, 1891, 10,231

University of Illinois at Chicago, Chicago, 1965, 24,985; *at Urbana-Champaign,* Urbana, 1867, 35,815

Western Illinois University, Macomb, 1899, 13,377

Wheaton College, Wheaton, 1860, 2,606

Where To Get More Information

Illinois Dept. of Commerce and Community Affairs 620 East Adams St. Springfield, IL 62701 or call, 800-223-0121

Iowa

The state seal of Iowa, adopted in 1847, is circular. In the center is a prairie scene: A pioneer citizen-soldier stands before a plow. In his right hand is an American flag with a liberty cap on top; in his left hand is a rifle. On the ground is a sheaf and a field of standing wheat, and a lead furnace and a pile of pig lead. In the distance is the Mississippi River, on which the steamer *Iowa* is sailing. An eagle flies above the scene with a banner in its beak. On the banner is the state motto. Around the seal is printed "The Great Seal of the State of Iowa."

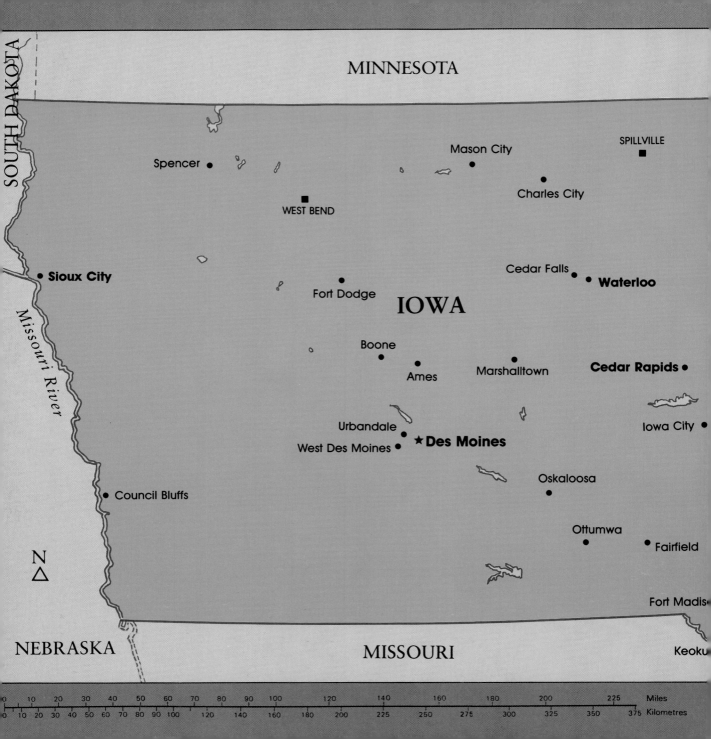

★ State Capital
● Cities or towns
■ OF SPECIAL INTEREST

WISCONSIN

EFFIGY MOUNDS
NATIONAL MONUMENT

Dubuque ●

Clinton ●

EST BRANCH

Davenport ● Bettendorf ●

● Muscatine

■ MARK TWAIN NATIONAL
WILDLIFE REFUGE

Mississippi River

lington

ILLINOIS

Capital: Des Moines

State Flag

State Bird: Eastern Goldfinch

State Flower:
Wild Rose

Major Crops:
Corn, soybeans,
oats, hay

Size: 56,275 square miles (25th largest)
Population: 2,812,448 (30th largest)

State Flag

Designed by Mrs. Dixie Cornell Gebhardt and adopted in 1921, the state flag of Iowa consists of three broad vertical stripes of blue, white, and red. In the center of the white stripe is the eagle and banner from the state seal with the word "Iowa" printed below it.

State Motto

Our Liberties We Prize, and Our Rights We Will Maintain

Adopted in 1846, the motto expresses the feelings of the people of the state as they entered the Union.

Hot-air ballooning is a popular sport in Iowa, where the view from above is endless.

State Name and Nickname

The Iowa River was named for the Iowa Indians who lived in the area, and the state was named after the river. The Indian word was *Ayuxwa*, which meant "one who puts to sleep." It was spelled by French explorers as "Ayoua" and by the English as "Ioway."

Although it is unofficial, the nickname for the state is the *Hawkeye State*, a tribute to the Indian chief Black Hawk.

State Capital

The first capital of Iowa was Burlington (1838-41). Iowa City became the capital in 1841, and Des Moines in 1857. The capitol building in Des Moines was first occupied in 1884. It has a steel and stone dome covered with gold leaf, and was constructed of Iowa stone, Iowa granite, Missouri limestone, and anamosa from Iowa, Ohio, Minnesota, and Illinois. The original cost of the building was $2,873,294.

State Flower

In 1897, the wild rose, *Rosa pratincola*, was named the state flower of Iowa.

State Tree

The white oak, *Quercus alba*, was designated the state tree in 1961.

State Bird

The eastern goldfinch, *Spinus tristis*, was adopted as state bird in 1933.

State Rock

The geode, a hollow stone with crystals at the center, was named state rock in 1967

State Songs

"The Song of Iowa," with words set to "Der Tannenbaum" by S. H. M. Byers, was adopted as the state song in 1911. An unofficial state song is the "Iowa Corn Song" by George Hamilton.

Population

The population of Iowa in 1992 was 2,812,448, making it the 30th most populous state. There are 50.3 persons per square mile.

Industries

The principal industries in Iowa are wholesale and retail trade, insurance, finance and real estate, and agriculture. The chief manufactured products are tires, farm machinery, electronic products, appliances, office furniture, chemicals, fertilizers, and auto accessories.

Agriculture

The chief crops of the state are silage, grain corn, soybeans, oats, and hay. Iowa is also a livestock state, and there are estimated to be some 4.45 million cattle, 15 million hogs and pigs, 345,000 sheep and lambs, and 8.6 million turkeys on its farms. Red cedar trees are harvested. Crushed stone, cement, sand, and gravel are important mineral products.

Government

The governor of Iowa is elected to a four-year term, as are the other high executives of the state. The state legislature, called the general assembly, which meets annually, consists of a senate of 50 members and a house of representatives of 100 members, elected from 50 senatorial districts and 100 representative districts. The senators serve 4-year terms and the representatives 2-year terms. The most recent state constitution was adopted in 1857. In addition to its two U.S. senators, Iowa has five representatives in the U.S. House of Representatives. The state has seven votes in the electoral college.

Sports

Iowans have always been keenly interested in sports of all kinds. In 1883, the first American golf course opened in Burlington. The state is also unique in its fervid interest in girls' high school basketball, and, along with Oklahoma, is a hotbed for collegiate wrestling. In football, the University of Iowa won the Rose Bowl in 1957 and 1959.

Major Cities

Cedar Rapids (population 108,780). Settled in 1838, this city is located at the rapids of the Cedar River. It is one of the state's industrial leaders. Cereals, corn products, milk processing machinery, packaged meats, farm hardware, stock feeds, and electronic material are manufactured here.

Things to see in Cedar Rapids: Brucemore (1886), Czech Village, Cedar Rapids Museum of Art, Science Station, Five Seasons Center, Indian Creek Nature Center, Palisades-Kepler State Park, and Wapsipinicon State Park.

Davenport (population 95,333). Founded in 1808 along the Mississippi River, Davenport is part of the Quad Cities metropolitan area (which also includes Bettendorf and the Illinois

Iowa farmland is among the most fertile and productive in the country.

cities of Moline and Rock Island). It is a trading and manufacturing town, and here are produced machinery, agricultural goods, and food products.

Things to see in Davenport: Davenport Museum of Art, Putnam Museum, Fejervary Park Zoo, Vander Veer Park, West Lake Park, and Scott County Park

Located in West Bend, the Grotto of Redemption was made with stones from every state of the Union and portrays man's fall from grace and redemption.

Des Moines (population 193,189). Founded in 1843, the capital city is also the industrial, retailing, financial, and insurance capital of the state. It was originally a fort on the Raccoon and Des Moines rivers, and was opened to settlers in 1845.

Things to see in Des Moines:
State Capitol (1871), Des Moines Art Center, Science Center of Iowa, Polk County Heritage Gallery, Salisbury House, Terrace Hill (1869), Heritage Village, Blank Park Zoo, Botanical Center and the Living History Farms.

Sioux City (population 80,505). Founded in 1854 by John K. Cook and incorporated in 1857, it is the industrial and commercial center of the area. It has a livestock market and meat-packing center and its manufactured goods include trucks, tractors, automobile accessories, foundry and machine products, tools, and fertilizers. Located in western Iowa at the head of navigation on the Missouri River, it is at the junction of the Iowa, Nebraska, and South Dakota borders.

Things to see in Sioux City:
Sioux City Art Center and the Sioux City Public Museum.

Places to Visit

The National Park Service maintains two areas in the state of Iowa: Effigy Mounds National Monument and Herbert Hoover National Historic Site. In addition, there are 65 state recreation areas.

Amana Colonies: Museum of Amana History. The exhibits include a nursery school, crafts and trades, and other items in the history of the Amana Colonies, a communal religious group.

Cedar Falls: Ice House Museum. A round icehouse in which cut natural ice was stored and sold. It also has displays, equipment, and memorabilia.

Decorah: Vesterheim, the Norwegian-American Museum. Exhibits explain the story of the Norwegians in the United States.

Dubuque: Woodward Riverboat Museum. Exhibits explain 300 years of Mississippi River history.

The skyline of Des Moines, Iowa's largest city.

Elk Horn: Danish Windmill. This working windmill was built in Denmark in 1848, and shipped to Iowa.

Fort Dodge: Fort Dodge Historical Museum, Stockade and Fort. A replica of the 1862 fort.

Fort Madison: Lee County Courthouse. Built in 1841, this is the oldest courthouse in continuous use in Iowa.

Indianola: National Balloon Museum. A collection of balloon memorabilia from the Balloon Federation of America is housed here.

Iowa City: Old Capitol. The first capitol of Iowa has been restored to its original appearance.

Newton: Trainland, USA. This toy train museum shows the development of American railroads.

Pella: Pella Historical Village Museum. Twenty restored buildings, including Wyatt Earp's boyhood home, can be visited.

Events

There are many events and organizations that schedule activities of various kinds in the state of Iowa. Here are some of them.

Sports: Creston Hot-Air Balloon Days (Creston), Drake Relays (Des Moines), Tri-State Rodeo (Fort Madison), National Balloon Classic (Indianola), Old Capitol Criterium Bicycle Race (Iowa City), Amana VIP Golf Tournament (Iowa City), Iowa Pro Hot Air Balloon Championship (Oskaloosa), Ottumwa Pro Balloon Races (Ottumwa), Balloon Days (Storm Lake).

Arts and Crafts: Art-a-Fest/Heritage-Fest (Charles City), Antique Show (Fort Madison).

Iowa City is the site of the state's "Old Capitol."

Music: Summerfest (Ames), Band Concerts (Cedar Falls), Glenn Miller Festival (Clarinda), Southwest Iowa Band Jamboree (Clarinda), Bix Beiderbecke Jazz Festival (Davenport), Music on the March (Dubuque), Des Moines Metro Opera (Indianola), Octoberfest of Bands (Maquoketa).

Entertainment: Veishea Spring Festival (Ames), Pufferbilly Days (Boone), Burlington Steamboat Days and the American Music Festival (Burlington), Sturgis Falls Days Celebration (Cedar Falls), All-Iowa Fair (Cedar Rapids), Riverboat Days (Clinton), Great Mississippi Valley Fair (Davenport), Nordic Fest (Decorah), Two Rivers Festival (Des Moines), Iowa State Fair (Des Moines), Dubuque Fest (Dubuque), Winter Sports Festival (Estherville), Kalona Fall Festival (Iowa City), North Iowa Fair (Mason City), Midwest Old Settlers and Threshers Reunion (Mount Pleasant), Southern Iowa Fair (Oskaloosa), Tulip Festival (Pella), River-Cade Festival (Sioux City), Flagfest Summer Festival (Spencer), Santa's Village (Storm Lake), Mesquakie Indian Powwow (Tama), National Cattle Congress (Waterloo), Covered Bridge Festival (Winterset).

Theater: Riverview Park (Clinton), Okoboji Summer Theater (Okoboji).

The sun sets over one of Iowa's many bogs.

The Land and the Climate

Most of Iowa is a gently rolling plain, rising almost imperceptibly from the east to the west. Much of it was once part of the vast natural prairie that extended from eastern Illinois to the foothills of the Rockies, where high prairie grass covered some of the richest soil in the world.

During the Ice Age, four glaciers moved over the land that is now Iowa, cutting off the tops of hills and filling valleys with the rich topsoil that is so much a part of the Corn Belt. Three separate land regions were formed in what would become Iowa.

The Dissected Till Plains cover the southern region of the state and run along the western border. The glaciers deposited till (layers of soil and rocks), which was later cut into (dissected) by streams that formed many low rolling hills and ridges. Then winds spread the fertile soil over these hills and ridges and piled it up along the edge of the Missouri River to the west, forming bluffs that rise from 100 to 300 feet above that river.

The Young Drift Plains cover most of northern and central Iowa. Three of the glaciers moved across this area, leveling the land and leaving behind many lakes and swamps. The lakes remain, but the swamps have been drained and turned into fine farmland producing such crops as corn, oats, soybeans, and hay. Dairy products and poultry are other important farm products here.

The Driftless Area starts in the northeast corner of the state, following the Mississippi River about halfway down the eastern border. Only one glacier moved across this region, so the area was not flattened as much as other portions of Iowa. Here are found rugged, pine-covered hills and cliffs: Iowans call the region "the Switzerland of America." However, its soil is the least favorable in the state for farming.

Wide, flat, open spaces are characteristic of most of the land in Iowa.

Far left:
Corn is Iowa's major crop. Here a harvesting machine cuts down the corn so farmer can separate the ears from th stalks.

After the corn is cut, it is col lected and is either used as animal feed or sent to marke for human consumption.

A view of Iowa's gently rolling farmland. The exceptionally rich topsoil under the prairie grass attracted many settlers to the state in the 1850s.

Many glaciers moved across the region that is now Iowa, leveling the land and leaving behind large lakes and rivers.

Only one glacier moved across the Driftless Area, leaving much of the land hilly, rocky, and heavily wooded like this section of Backbone State Park.

An Iowa winter scene.

Iowa is the only state to be bordered by two navigable rivers—the Mississippi to the east and the Missouri to the west. The Des Moines River flows diagonally northwest to southeast, emptying into the Mississippi, as do the Iowa and Cedar Rivers. Small, beautiful lakes dot the countryside of northern and northwestern Iowa, including Clear, Okoboji, Spirit, Storm, and West Lakes.

Iowa has a humid, mid–American climate—cold winters with heavy snowfalls, hot summers, and rainy springs. Temperature changes are sudden and temperature extremes are common. Winter temperatures below zero degrees F. and summer temperatures above 100 degrees F. are not unusual. Rainfall ranges from 26 to 36 inches. The average January temperature in Des Moines is 20 degrees F.; the average July temperature is 75 degrees F.

The History

As was the case in Illinois, the prehistoric Indians called Mound Builders were the first residents of Iowa, and they disappeared long before the white man came to the region. The Mound Builders left more than 10,000 burial mounds—elaborate earthworks containing tools and weapons. Then came both Woodland and Plains Indians. The Illinois, Iowa, Miami, Ottawa, and Sioux lived along the Mississippi, and the Omaha, Oto, and Missouri tribes lived in the western part of the state. After 1733, Sauk and Fox Indians moved in from Wisconsin under pressure from the French.

As happened throughout the Midwest, the first white men to come to this area were French trappers and explorers. Two explorers, Father Jacques Marquette and Louis Joliet, paddled their canoes down the Wisconsin River into the Mississippi in 1673, landing on the Iowa side. In 1680 Robert Cavelier, Sieur de la Salle, sent Michel Aco and Father Louis Hennepin to explore the upper Mississippi, and they passed by the Iowa shore. La Salle headed south, reaching the mouth of the Mississippi, and claimed for France the entire region drained by the river, naming it Louisiana in honor of King Louis XIV.

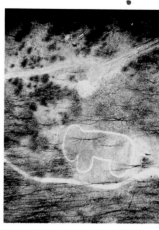

This photograph shows the area in which the prehistoric tribe called the Mound Builders built effigy mounds. The mounds remain to this day as valuable evidence of the Mound Builder culture.

An 1859 engraving of Dubuque, one of the largest cities in Iowa. The city was named for the explorer Julien Dubuque, one of the first white men to settle in the state.

Fur traders began to follow these explorers, although most of them headed farther west. For the next few years only a few missionaries, fur traders, and soldiers visited the area. In 1762 France gave Spain control of the Louisiana Territory west of the Mississippi. In 1788 Julien Dubuque, a French-Canadian adventurer, became one of the first white men to settle in Iowa. He had received permission from the Fox Indians to mine lead near what is now the city named for him.

In 1800 Spain returned its part of Louisiana to France, and in 1803 Iowa was included in the Louisiana Purchase, whereby the United States bought 828,000 square miles of land from France for $15,000,000. Two years later the Federal Government created the Territory of Louisiana, which included Iowa. The U.S. Army built Iowa's first fort, Fort Madison, in 1808. When Louisiana became a state in 1812, Iowa became part of the Territory of Missouri. Then Missouri became a state (1821) and Iowa was an unorganized territory for some time. After the Black Hawk War in Illinois in 1832, the Sauk and Fox Indians, who had fought under Chief Black Hawk, were forced to move out of a 50-mile strip of land along the Mississippi in Iowa. Many settlers moved into it, and the strip became part of the Territory of Michigan.

In 1838 Congress created the Territory of Iowa, which included that strip known as the Black Hawk Purchase. The territory included all of Iowa, most of Minnesota, and parts of North and South Dakota. Finally, in 1846, Iowa became the 29th state of the Union, with Ansel Briggs as its governor. By 1850, after the prairie grass had been cleared to reveal an unusually rich topsoil, there were nearly 200,000 people in the state; by 1860, nearly 700,000. New Englanders had been lured there to farm the soil that was so much richer than that of the Northeast. Scottish miners came to work the coal mines. A German religious community, the Amana Society, established several towns, and people came in from Ireland, Norway, Sweden, the Netherlands, Denmark, and Czechoslovakia—many of them setting up ethnic towns that cling to their heritage even today. The last significant

A bakery built by the German Amana Society, which was one [of] the first ethnic groups to establi[sh] towns in the state.

resistance from the native peoples came in 1857, when the Sioux attacked and killed 40 settlers at Spirit Lake.

Iowa supported the Union during the Civil War. In 1867 came the first railroad train to cross the state from the Mississippi River to Council Bluffs. Steamboating became a giant industry on the Mississippi. In the early 1900s, new dams were built to provide power, and Iowa was established as a major transportation, energy, and farming state whose principal crop was corn.

Then came World War I. Private Merle Hay of Glidden, Iowa, was one of the first American soldiers to be killed in battle overseas, and France erected a monument in his honor. The Great Depression of the 1930s left its mark next: by 1935 more than half the state's farmers had lost their land. (Many had gone deeply into debt to buy more land during the prosperous years that followed World War I.) However, with World War II came a huge demand for American farm products (1939–1945) and many Iowa farmers were saved by supplying corn and pork to Allied armies and civilians as well. They also formed cooperatives to buy and sell their goods at lower cost. After the war, Iowa began to industrialize, and thousands of new manufacturing plants were built.

In the early 1980s, falling crop prices left Iowa farmers unable to pay loans they had secured in the financially sound 1970s. Between 1978 and 1983, over 10,000 Iowa farms went out of business. In 1985, Governor Terry Branstad declared a state of emergency and temporarily stopped farm foreclosures. A severe drought in 1988 resulted in another state of emergency when Iowa experienced its lowest corn and soybean harvests since 1974. Iowa has diversified its economy by increasing manufacturing, but the items produced in this region are farming-related and production suffers when farm revenues decline. In 1991, small-scale casino gambling on Mississippi River paddleboats was legalized to attract tourists and to stimulate the economy.

Today, Iowa represents a welding of divergent ethnic groups into a common social and economic order. It is perhaps one of the most typically American of all the states, combining urban and rural areas for a healthy balance of industry and agriculture.

Education

Iowa's earliest school, founded in 1830, was a private school for settler's children. In 1965, a law established a system of community colleges so that each county had a representative school. The oldest state institution of higher learning is the University of Iowa in Iowa City, chartered in 1847. Iowa Wesleyan College at Mount Pleasant (1842) is Iowa's oldest private institution of higher education.

The People

About 44 percent of Iowans live in metropolitan areas. Approximately 80 percent of Iowa residents were born in the state and about 98 percent were born in the United States. One-third of the residents who were born in foreign countries came from Germany. Protestant churches have the largest combined membership in the state, although the Roman Catholic Church forms the largest single religious group.

Bob Feller was a Hall of Fame pitcher who compiled a record of 266 wins and 162 losses over 18 years with the Cleveland Indians.

Famous People

Many famous people were born in the state of Iowa. Here are a few:

Fran Allison 1908-1989, La Porte City. Television hostess of *Kukla, Fran and Ollie*

Cap Anson 1852-1922, Marshalltown. Hall of Fame baseball player

Bix Beiderbecke 1903-1931, Davenport. Jazz cornetist

Eugene Burdick 1918-1965, Sheldon. Novelist: *The Ugly American, Fail-Safe*

Johnny Carson b. 1925, Corning. Television host

Marquis Childs 1903-90, Clinton. Pulitzer Prize–winning columnist

Buffalo Bill Cody 1846-1917, Scott County. Army scout and showman

Mamie Eisenhower 1896-1979, Boone. First lady

Bob Feller b. 1918, Van Meter. Hall of Fame baseball pitcher

Frank J. Fletcher 1885-1973, Marshalltown. World War II admiral

Janet Guthrie b. 1938, Iowa City. Auto racer

James Hall 1887-1951, Colfax. Novelist: *Mutiny on the Bounty, Men Against the Sea*

Herbert Hoover 1874-1964, West Branch. Thirty-first President of the United States

MacKinlay Kantor 1904-1977, Webster City. Pulitzer Prize-winning novelist: *Andersonville, Long Remember*

Ann Landers b. 1918, Sioux City. Advice columnist

Cloris Leachman b. 1926, Des Moines. Academy Award-winning actress: *The Last Picture Show, Young Frankenstein*

John L. Lewis 1880-1969, Lucas. Union leader

Elmer H. Maytag 1883-1940, Newton. Appliance manufacturer

Glenn Miller 1904-1944, Clarinda. Band leader and trombonist

Harriet Nelson b. 1914, Des Moines. Television actress: *The Adventures of Ozzie and Harriet*

John S. Phillips 1861-1949, Council Bluffs. Magazine publisher

Harry Reasoner 1923-91, Dakota City. Television news correspondent

Donna Reed 1921-1986,

Denison. Academy Award-winning actress: *From Here to Eternity*, *It's A Wonderful Life*

Lillian Russell 1861-1921, Clinton. Vaudeville singer and actress

Jacob Schick 1877-1937, Des Moines. Shaver manufacturer

Billy Sunday 1862-1935, Ames. Evangelist

Abigail Van Buren b. 1918, Sioux City. Advice columnist

John Wayne 1907-79, Winterset. Academy Award-winning actor: *True Grit*, *The Shootist*

Andy Williams b. 1930, Wall Lake. Pop singer

Meredith Willson 1902-84, Mason City. Tony Award-winning composer: *The Music Man*, *The Unsinkable Molly Brown*

Grant Wood 1892-1942, Anamosa. Painter

Colleges and Universities
There are many colleges and universities in Iowa. Here are the more prominent, with their locations, dates of founding, and enrollments.

Briar Cliff College, Sioux City, 1930, 1,144

Buena Vista College, Storm Lake, 1891, 971

Clarke College, Dubuque, 1843, 903

Coe College, Cedar Rapids, 1851, 1,285

Cornell College, Mount Vernon, 1853, 1,162

Drake University, Des Moines, 1881, 6,333

Graceland College, Lamoni, 1895, 1,058

Grinnell College, Grinnell, 1846, 1,240

Iowa State University of Science and Technology, Ames, 1858, 25,263

Iowa Wesleyan College, Mount Pleasant, 1842, 994

Loras College, Dubuque, 1839, 1,776

Luther College, Decorah, 1861, 2,327

Morningside College, Sioux City, 1894, 1,288

Mount Mercy College, Cedar Rapids, 1928, 1,398

Northwestern College, Orange City, 1882, 1,055

St. Ambrose College, Davenport, 1882, 2,417

Simpson College, Indianola, 1860, 1,690

University of Dubuque, Dubuque, 1852, 1,264

University of Iowa, Iowa City, 1847, 27,463

University of Northern Iowa, Cedar Falls, 1876, 13,045

Wartburg College, Waverly, 1852, 1,445

Where To Get More Information
The Tourism Bureau of the Department of Economic Development
200 East Grand Avenue
Des Moines, IA 50309
Or Call 1-800-345 IOWA

Minnesota

The state seal of Minnesota was adopted in 1858. It is circular, and on it is a rural scene, with a farmer plowing a field and an Indian riding a horse toward the setting sun. In the distance are a waterfall and a forest. In the foreground is the farmer's rifle and powderhorn leaning against a stump. Above the picture is a banner bearing the state motto. Surrounding the picture is printed "The Great Seal of the State of Minnesota" and "1858"—the date of the state's entry into the Union.

NORTHERNMOST PART OF
THE UNITED STATES
OUTSIDE OF ALASKA

CANADA

★ State Capital
● Cities or towns
■ OF SPECIAL INTEREST

RED LAKE
INDIAN RESERVATION

NETT LAKE
INDIAN RESERVATION

SUPERIOR
NATIONAL FOREST

CHIPPEWA
NATIONAL FOREST

LEECH LAKE
INDIAN RESERVATION

HIBBING

LAKE
SUPERIOR

NORTH DAKOTA

WHITE EARTH
INDIAN RESERVATION

●Moorehead

FOND DU LAC
INDIAN RESERVATION

●Duluth

MICHIGAN

BRAINERD

MINNESOTA

WISCONSIN

Saint Cloud

N
△

SOUTH DAKOTA

Minnesota River

Minneapolis● ★Saint Paul

MENDOTA

Mississippi River

Mankato

Rochester

Winona

●Austin

IOWA

0 10 20   40   60   80   100   120   140   160   180   200   225   250   275   300   325 Miles
0 10 20   40   60   80   100 120 140 160 180 200 225 250 275 300 325 350 375 400 425 450 475 500 525 Kilometres

MINNESOTA
At a Glance

Capital: St. Paul

State Flag

Major Industries: Agriculture, food processing, mining, lumbering

Major Crops: Corn, soybeans, wheat, barley

Size: 84,402 square miles (12th largest)
Population: 4,480,034 (20th largest)

State Bird: Common Loon

State Flower: Pink and White Lady's Slipper

51

State Flag

The state flag, adopted in 1957, contains a white circle with a yellow border on a field of blue. Inside the circle, scenes from the state seal are reproduced in full color. Underneath is the word "Minnesota", and surrounding the scene are 19 stars, representing Minnesota's place as the 19th state to be admitted after the original 13.

State Motto

L'Etoile du Nord

The French motto means "Star of the North," and was approved in 1861.

The beauty and solitude of Tuscarora Lake.

State Capital

St. Paul was named the capital city in 1849, and Minnesota has had no other capital.

State Name and Nicknames

In the language of the Dakota Indians, the name of the Minnesota River was *Mnishota*, which means "cloudy (or milky) water." The state took its name from the river.

Because of its motto, Minnesota is often called the *North Star State*. Other nicknames are the *Land of 10,000 Lakes* (although it has far more than that), the *Gopher State* (for the many gophers that used to be found on the prairies), and the *Bread and Butter State* (because of its production of wheat and dairy products).

State Flower

The pink-and-white lady slipper, *Cypripedium reginae*, was named the state flower of Minnesota in 1902.

State Tree

The Norway pine, *Pinus resinosa*, was adopted as state tree in 1953.

State Bird

In 1961, the common loon, *Gavia immer*, was selected as state bird.

State Drink

Because of the importance of the dairy industry, milk was selected as state drink in 1984.

State Fish

The walleye, *Stizostedion vitreum*, was named the state fish in 1965.

State Gem

The Lake Superior agate has been the state gem since 1969.

State Grain

Selected in 1977, wild rice, *Zizania aquatica*, is the state grain.

State Mushroom

The morel, *Morchella esculenta*, is the state mushroom, and was adopted in 1984.

State Song

Named in 1945, the state song of Minnesota is "Hail! Minnesota," with music by Truman E. Rickard and words by Truman E. Rickard and Arthur E. Upson.

Population

The population of Minnesota in 1992 was 4,480,034, making it the 20th most populous state. There are 56.3 persons per square mile.

Industries

The principal industries of the state of Minnesota are farming, forest products, mining, and tourism. The chief manufactured products are processed foods, non-electrical machinery, chemicals, paper, electric and electronic equipment, printing and publishing, instruments, and fabricated metal products.

Agriculture

The chief crops of the state are corn, soybeans, wheat, sugar beets, sunflowers, and barley. Minnesota is also a livestock state, and there are estimated to be some 2.95 million cattle, 4.25 million hogs and pigs, 285,000 sheep, and 12.7 million chickens and turkeys on its farms. Needled and hardwood trees are harvested. Iron ore, sand, gravel, and crushed stone are important mineral resources. Commercial fishing earned $101,000 in 1992.

Government

The governor of Minnesota is elected to a four-year term, as are the lieutenant governor, secretary of state, attorney general, treasurer, and auditor. The state legislature, which meets for a total of 120 days within every two years, consists of a 67-member senate and a 134-member house of representatives. The senators serve four-year terms, and are elected from 67 legislative districts. The representatives serve two-year terms, and from one to three are elected from the 67 legislative districts, depending on population. The most recent state constitution was adopted in 1858. In addition to its two U.S. senators, Minnesota has eight representatives in the U.S. House of Representatives. The state has ten votes in the electoral college.

Sports

Minnesota is a sports state, and many of its residents are skiing enthusiasts. On the collegiate level, the University of Minnesota has won the NCAA national hockey championship (1974, 1976, 1979), the NCAA national baseball championship (1956, 1960, 1964), and the Rose Bowl football game (1962).

On the professional level, the Minnesota Twins defeated the St. Louis Cardinals to win their first World Series in 1987, and they won their second title in 1991 against the Atlanta Braves. The Twins of the American League play baseball in the Hubert H. Humphrey Metrodome in Minneapolis. They share this facility with the Minnesota Vikings of the National Football League. The Minnesota Timberwolves of the National Basketball Association play their games in Target Center in Minneapolis, while the Minnesota North Stars of the National Hockey League play in the Metropolitan Sports Center in Bloomington.

The scenic cliffs of North Shore at Palisade Head.

Duluth (population 85,493). Founded in 1856, Duluth is a world port located at the western tip of Lake Superior. It is one of the greatest grain-exporting cities in the country, and it also ships iron ore, coal, limestone, crude oil, and many other products. Duluth is a business, industrial, cultural, recreational, and vacation center.

Things to see in Duluth:
Aerial Lift Bridge, Corps of Engineers Canal Park Marine Museum, Fitger's on the Lake, Leif Erickson Park,

The skyscrapers of Minneapolis, the largest city in the state. The city sits next to the capital St. Paul.

Duluth Zoological Gardens, Skyline Parkway Drive, Enger Tower, Glensheen (1905-08), St. Louis County Heritage and Arts Center, Depot Square, A. M. Chisholm Museum, St. Louis County Historical Society, Lake Superior Museum of Transportation, Tweed Museum of Art, and Marshall W. Alworth Planetarium.

Minneapolis (population 368,383). Settled in 1847, Minnesota's largest city is located on the Mississippi River. Even with its skyscrapers, parks, and industry, it still has a frontier vigor. Its name comes from the Sioux word minne, meaning "water," and the Greek *polis*, meaning "city."

Things to see in Minneapolis:
Nicollet Mall, IDS Tower, St. Anthony Falls, Minnehaha Park, Minneapolis Institute of Arts, Walker Art Center, Bell Museum of Natural History, American Swedish Institute, Minneapolis Grain Exchange, Minneapolis City Hall (1891), Minneapolis Planetarium, Hennepin County Historical Society Museum, Minnesota Transportation Museum,

Lyndale Park, Eloise Butler Wildflower Garden and Bird Sanctuary, and Minnesota Zoo.

St. Paul (population 272,235). Settled in 1840, the capital of Minnesota began as a settlement known as Pig's Eye. There are 90 parks and 30 lakes within a 30-minute drive from the city. It is located across the Mississippi River from Minneapolis.

Things to see in St. Paul:
State Capitol (1896-1905), Minnesota Historical Society, City Hall and Courthouse (1932), Landmark Center, Northwest Center Skyway, Science Museum of Minnesota, Minnesota Museum of Art, Children's Museum, James J. Hill Mansion (1891), Alexander Ramsey House (1872), Gibbs Farm Museum (1854), Town Square Park, Como Park, Indian Mounds Park, and Historic Fort Snelling.

Places to Visit

The National Park Service maintains seven areas in the state of Minnesota: Pipestone National Monument, Grand Portage National Monument,

Voyageurs National Park, St. Croix National Scenic Riverway, Lower St. Croix National Riverway, Chippewa National Forest, and Superior National Forest. In addition, there are 70 state recreation areas.

Alexandria: Kensington Runestone Museum. A sandstone boulder with runic inscriptions dated 1362 (said to be Viking) is the most important exhibit.

Bemidji: Paul Bunyan and Blue Ox. Giant replicas of Bunyan and "Babe," his pet, are on display.

Brainerd: Lumbertown, USA. A replica of an old-time lumber town, it contains a store, school, saloon, and more.

Elk River: Oliver H. Kelley Farm and Interpretive Center. This living-history farm was the birthplace of the National Grange.

Eveleth: U.S. Hockey Hall of Fame. The museum honors American players and the sport.

Grand Portage: Grand Portage National Monument. This is a partially restored fur-trading post.

Hibbing: Hull-Rust Mahoning Mine. One of the largest open-pit iron mines, it

Indians perform a ceremony with a peace pipe in the annual Grand Portage Pow Wow.

stretches for three miles and is known as the "Grand Canyon of Minnesota."

International Falls: Smokey the Bear Statue. This is a giant symbol for the campaign against forest fires.

Little Falls: Charles A. Lindbergh House and Interpretive Center. This was the boyhood home of the aviator.

Mankato: Blue Earth County Historical Society. Indian and pioneer exhibits are housed in an 1871 Victorian mansion.

Moorhead: Heritage-Hjemkomst Interpretive Center. A Viking ship replica is one of the major exhibits.

Sauk Centre: Sinclair Lewis Boyhood Home. The restored home of the Nobel Prize-winning novelist.

Shakopee: Valleyfair. This is a turn-of-the-century theme amusement park.

Tracy: Laura Ingalls Wilder Museum and Tourist Center. The museum, a tribute to the novelist, is in an old railroad depot.

Two Harbors: Lake County Historical and Railroad

Museum. The museum in a depot features old locomotives, including a 1941 Mallet.

Events

There are many events and organizations that schedule activities of various kinds in the state of Minnesota. Here are some of them.

Sports: Operation Jumpfest (Albert Lea), Arabian Horse Show (Albert Lea), Brainerd International Raceway (Brainerd), John Beargrease Sled Dog Marathon (Duluth), All-American Championship Sled Dog Races (Ely), "Wilderness Trek" (Ely), Scout Fishing Derby (Glenwood), Last Chance Curling Bonspiel (Hibbing), Jackson National Sprint Car Races (Jackson), International Rolle Bolle Tournament (Marshall), Aquatennial Festival (Minneapolis), Vasaloppet-Cross-Country Ski Race (Mora), Muskie Northern Derby Days (Walker).

Arts and Crafts: Blueberry/Art Festival (Ely).

Music: Scandinavian Folkfest (Detroit Lakes), WE Country Music Fest (Detroit Lakes), Lake Superior Old Time Fiddler's Contest (Duluth), International Folk Festival (Duluth), New Dance Ensemble (Minneapolis), Minnesota Orchestra (Minneapolis), Sommerfest (Minneapolis), The Glockenspiel (New Ulm), The Rochester Carillon (Rochester), Rochester Symphony Orchestra (Rochester), Minnesota Opera Company (St. Paul), St. Paul Chamber Orchestra (St. Paul), Sonshine Festival (Willmar).

Entertainment: Halloween Festival (Anoka), National Barrow Show (Austin), Paul Bunyan Water Carnival (Bemidji), Lumberjack Days (Cloquet), Red River Valley Winter Shows (Crookston), Northwest Water Carnival (Detroit Lakes), Soo Line Days (Glenwood), Fisherman's Picnic (Grand Marais), Judy Garland Festival (Grand Rapids), Tall Timber Days and U.S. Chainsaw Carving Championships (Grand Rapids), Itasca County Fair (Grand Rapids), Rivertown Days (Hastings), Ethnic Days (Hibbing), Ice Box Days (International Falls), Renaissance Festival (Minneapolis), Victorian Christmas (Minneapolis), Prairie Pioneer Days (Morris), Fasching (New Ulm), Heritagefest (New Ulm), Defeat of Jesse James Days (Northfield), Perham Pioneer Festival (Perham), River City Days (Red Wing), Minnesota Inventors Congress (Redwood Falls), Winter Carnival (St. Paul), Macalester College Scottish Country Fair (St. Paul), Minnesota State Fair (St. Paul), Winterfest (Sauk Centre), Sinclair Lewis Days (Sauk Centre), Ag Days and Corn Feed (Spring Valley), Lumberjack Days (Stillwater), Box Car Days (Tracy), Eelpout Festival (Walker), Steamboat Days (Winona), Weekend Wildlife Show (Winona), Victorian Fair (Winona), King Turkey Days and Great Gobbler Gallop (Worthington).

Theater: Paul Bunyan Playhouse (Bemidji), Mississippi Melodie Showboat (Grand Rapids), Guthrie Theater (Minneapolis), Showboat (Minneapolis), University Theatre (Minneapolis).

Minnesota's cold and snowy climate is conducive to cross-country skiing.

A dazzling array of lights and ice sculptures adorn the plaza at Rice Park in St. Paul.

Along Minnesota's western border the land is flat and very fertile.

Minnesota is known as "the land of a thousand lakes."

The terrain of Blue Mound State Park is a good example of the rock formations typical of the Superior Upland in the northeast part of the state.

The Land and the Climate

The last Ice-Age glacier that moved across Minnesota retreated from the area about 12,000 years ago. Only a small region in the southeast was untouched by these massive ice floes, which leveled the land and created hills and lakes, swamps and marshes. Today, the state has four major land regions.

The Superior Upland, with its hard rock formations, is in the northeast part of the state, covering an area from about halfway up the eastern border almost to the western border. It is here that most of Minnesota's iron ore deposits are found, as well as the highest point in the state—Eagle Mountain, at 2,301 feet.

The Young Drift Plains contain rolling farmland and extend in a strip along the western border, widening to the southern border and extending to the eastern border. The glaciers deposited much fertile topsoil, called drift, as they melted. This region includes the best farmland in Minnesota and countless lakes carved out by glacial activity.

The Dissected Till Plains cover a small portion of the southeast corner of the state. Here the sand, gravel and clay (together called till) deposited by the glaciers was cut up by numerous streams.

The Driftless Area, where soil is sparser, is in the southeastern corner of Minnesota, along the Mississippi River. This region was not glaciated, but streams cut deep valleys in the eastern part. The western part is almost flat.

The climate of Minnesota is continental, or mid-American, with extremely cold winters and, occasionally, very hot periods during the summer. Temperature changes can be sudden and severe. Most of the northern part of the state is snow-covered for more than four months in the winter. Rainfall ranges from 25 to 29 inches per year, and the annual snowfall is about 42 inches. Average temperatures range from 8 degrees F. in January to 72 degrees F. in July.

Northern Minnesota often remains covered with snow for more than four months in the winter.

Southeast Minnesota land contains a high percentage of sand, gravel, and clay and is not well-suited to farming. The rocky hills and denser foliage give this area a look that is distinct from that of the rest of the state.

Minnesotans take advantage of the long, snowy winters by sledding, racing dogsleds, cross-country skiing, and ice-skating. Many of the foreign-born immigrants to Minnesota came from northern European countries, like Norway, Finland and Sweden, with a similarly cold climate.

A tepee standing at Pipestone National Monument. Indians have played a large part in Minnesota's history.

The History

French trappers and missionaries, entering the region that is now Minnesota from the Great Lakes, began to arrive in 1659, but established no settlements for many years. At that time there were Sioux Indians in the northern forests, living in dome-shaped wigwams, raising crops, and hunting game. Two French fur traders, Pierre Esprit Radisson and Médart Chouart, Sieur de Groseilliers, were probably the first white men to arrive, between 1659 and 1661. About 1796 Daniel Greysolon, Sieur Duluth (or Du Lhut), another Frenchman, came into Minnesota hoping to blaze a trail to the Pacific Ocean. Landing on the western shore of Lake Superior and pushing to the interior of the territory, he claimed the region in the name of King Louis XIV of France.

Minnesota's capital city of St. Paul in 1852.

Later, Father Louis Hennepin was captured by Indians in Illinois while exploring the Mississippi River. This Belgian missionary and his two companions were taken to Minnesota. Hennepin was the first white man to reach the site of present-day Minneapolis, where he discovered and named the Falls of St. Anthony. It was Duluth who freed Hennepin from the Indians.

The first settlement in the region—the village of Grand Portage—is believed to have been made by the French about 1730. But the French left few marks on the land, and in 1762 they gave all their claims west of the Mississippi River, including western Minnesota, to the Spanish. Since Spain did not explore or settle the area, French trappers continued to collect furs there. When the French and Indian Wars ended with the defeat of the French by the British in 1763, France gave England all of its land east of the Mississippi, including eastern Minnesota. During the next 50 years the North West Company and other British fur-trading firms established posts there.

At the end of the American Revolution, the British surrendered to the United States all their holdings south of the Great Lakes and east of the Mississippi. Not until after the Anglo-American War of 1812 did the United States gain control over eastern Minnesota. In the meantime, Napoleon had forced Spain to return the region west of the Mississippi to France, and the United States got control of northwestern Minnesota as part of the Louisiana Purchase from France in 1803. By this time Minnesota had been under four flags.

Sioux culture still thrives in many parts of Minnesota today. Here a Sioux woman works on a design for a piece of handmade pottery.

In 1851, under pressure from the U.S. Government, the Sioux signed two treaties by which they gave up their rights to millions of acres of land west of the Mississippi. Most of this land was in southern Minnesota, and the territory as we know it today was complete. On May 11, 1858, Minnesota was admitted to the Union as the 32nd state. Henry H. Sibley was elected governor of the 150,000 people who lived there.

When the Civil War began in 1861, Minnesota was the first state to offer troops for the Union Army. The following year, while many Minnesota men were away fighting the war, the Sioux made a last-ditch effort to regain their ancestral lands. They attacked the frontier towns, killing hundreds of settlers. Federal troops and Minnesota militiamen put down the uprising.

The railroads came in the late 1800s, the Sioux hunting grounds became wheat fields, and flour mills sprang up all over the state. During the 1880s and 1890s, thousands of Germans, Norwegians, and Swedes flocked to Minnesota to work on farms, in factories, and in iron mines.

When the United States entered World War I in 1917, there were heavy demands for Minnesota products—not only wheat and grains, but iron and steel. The Great Depression of the 1930s caused about 70 percent of the iron-range workers to lose their jobs, and many farmers lost their farms. World War II, however, created a big demand for the state's iron, crops, and lumber. Today, the state is prosperous, its balanced economy resting on the cornerstones of agriculture and heavy industry.

The majority of European immigrants who settled in Minnesota came from Scandinavian countries. The Nordic Festival pictured here is a regular chance for many Minnesotans to celebrate their family heritage.

Education

Common schools were established in Minnesota in 1849. A junior college system was implemented in 1957 and today there are 18 community colleges and 34 vocational-technical schools. There are 170 institutions of higher education, including 18 private institutions which originally had strong church ties. The University of Minnesota is one of the largest public university systems in the United States, with five campuses at Crookston, Duluth, Minneapolis-St.Paul, Morris, and Waseca.

A pow-wow of Grand Portage Indians. Many native Indian tribes remain a distinct part of modern-day Minnesota. The majority of the population is found on the four large Indian reservations in the northern half of the state.

The People

Almost two-thirds of the people in Minnesota live in cities. About 96 percent of them were born in the United States, and most of the few who were born in foreign countries came from Norway, Sweden, Denmark, and Finland—northern European countries whose climates and industries resemble those of Minnesota. The two largest religious groups in the state are the Roman Catholics and the Lutherans.

Famous People

Many famous people were born in the state of Minnesota. Here are a few:

Robert Bly b. 1926, Madison. Poet: *The Light Around the Body, Point Reyes Poems*

Warren E. Burger b. 1907, St. Paul. Supreme Court Chief Justice

William O. Douglas 1898-1980, Maine. Supreme Court justice

Bob Dylan b. 1941, Duluth. Folk singer

Richard G. Eberhart b. 1904, Austin. Pulitzer Prize-winning poet: *Selected Poems, Brotherhood of Men*

Mike Farrell b. 1939, St. Paul. Television actor: *M*A*S*H*

F. Scott Fitzgerald 1896-1940, St. Paul. Novelist: *The Great Gatsby, Tender Is the Night*

James Earle Fraser 1876-1953, Winona. Sculptor

Judy Garland 1922-1969, Grand Rapids. Academy Award-winning actress: *The Wizard of Oz,*

A Star Is Born

J. Paul Getty 1892-1976, Minneapolis. Oil company executive

Garrison Keillor b. 1942, Anoka. Writer and radio personality: *Lake Wobegon Days, A Prairie Home Companion*

Sinclair Lewis 1884-1951, Sauk Centre. Nobel Prize-wining novelist: *Elmer Gantry, Dodsworth*

F. Scott Fitzgerald was a novelist who wrote about people with wealth and privilege in the roaring 20's.

John Madden b. 1936, Austin. Professional football coach and television commentator

Roger Maris 1934-85, Hibbing. Baseball player

Charles Horace Mayo 1865-1939, Rochester. Co-founder of the Mayo Clinic

William James Mayo 1861-1939, Le Sueur. Co-founder of the Mayo Clinic

Eugene McCarthy b. 1916, Watkins. Presidential candidate

Kate Millett b. 1934, St. Paul. Feminist

Walter Mondale b. 1928, Ceylon. Presidential candidate

Ernie Nevers 1903-76, Willow River. Hall of Fame football player

Harrison E. Salisbury 1908-93, Minneapolis. Pulitzer Prize–winning newspaper correspondent

Charles Schulz b. 1922, Minneapolis. Creator of *Peanuts*

Richard W. Sears 1863-1914, Stewartville. Merchant

Harold E. Stassen b. 1907, St. Paul. Republican candidate for the presidency

De Witt Wallace 1889-1981, St. Paul. Founder of the *Reader's Digest*

Richard Widmark b. 1914, Sunrise. Film actor: *Kiss of Death, Against All Odds*

Colleges and Universities
There are many colleges and universities in Minnesota. Here are the more prominent, with their locations, dates of founding, and enrollments.

Augsburg College, Minneapolis, 1869, 2,924

Bemidji State University, Bemidji, 1919, 4,816

Bethel College, St. Paul, 1871, 1,963

Carleton College, Northfield, 1866, 1,662

College of Saint Benedict, Saint Joseph, 1887, 1,787

College of St. Catherine, St. Paul, 1905, 2,638

College of St. Scholastica, Duluth, 1912, 1,988

Concordia College, Moorhead, 1891, 2,942

Concordia College, St. Paul, 1893, 1,265

Gustavus Adolphus College, St. Peter, 1862, 2,275

Hamline University, St. Paul, 1854, 2,465

Macalester College, St. Paul, 1874, 1,838

Mankato State University, Mankato, 1867, 13,925

Moorhead State University, Moorhead, 1885, 8,723

St. Cloud State University, St. Cloud, 1869, 16,047

Saint John's University, Collegeville, 1857, 1,902

Saint Mary's College of Minnesota, Winona, 1912, 6,186

St. Olaf College, Northfield, 1874, 3,015

University of Minnesota at Duluth, Duluth, 1947, 7,680; *at Morris,* Morris, 1959, 1,923; *Twin Cities Campus,* Minneapolis, 1851, 38,019

Winona State University, Winona, 1858, 7,500

Where To Get More Information
Minnesota Travel Information Center
250 Skyway Level
375 Jackson Street
St. Paul, MN 55101

Wisconsin

FORWARD

The state seal of Wisconsin, adopted in 1851, is nearly identical to the state coat of arms pictured here. In the center is a shield with a plow in the upper left corner, a pick and shovel in the upper right, an anchor in the lower right, and an arm and hand holding a hammer in the lower left. These represent agriculture, mining, navigation, and industry. In the center of the shield is a smaller shield with the coat of arms of the United States, over which is printed *E Pluribus Unum,* Latin for "out of many, one"—the motto of the nation. To the left of the larger shield is a sailor holding a coil of rope, and on the right is a miner resting on his pick. Below the shield is a horn of plenty and a pyramid of pig lead. Above the shield is a badger. Over the badger is a banner with the word "Forward"—the state motto. In addition, the state seal has the words "Great Seal of the State of Wisconsin" at the top, and 13 stars on a banner at the bottom.

WISCONSIN
At a Glance

Capital: Madison

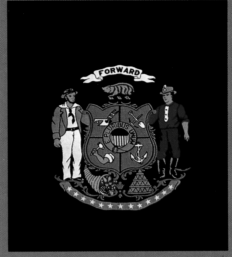

State Flag

State Flower: Wood Violet

Major Industries: Agriculture, dairy products, manufacturing, transportation

Size: 56,153 square miles
(26th largest)
Population: 5,006,591
(18th largest)

State Bird: Robin

State Motto: *Forward*
Nickname: The Badger State

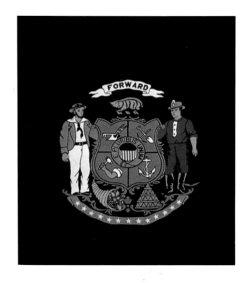

State Flag

The state flag contains the state seal on a blue background, with the word Wisconsin above it, and below it the date 1848, the year Wisconsin became a state. It was adopted in 1981.

State Motto

Forward

This motto became official in 1851.

Frank Lloyd Wright designed the House on the Rock.

State Capital

Before Wisconsin became a state, the capital of the territory was in Belmont (1836), Burlington (now in Iowa, 1837), and Madison (1838-48). Madison has been the capital ever since.

State Name and Nicknames

In Chippewa, *Wisconsin* meant "grassy place," and that is what the Indians called the Wisconsin River. The state was named after the river.

Although it is unofficial, the most common nickname of Wisconsin is the *Badger State*, named for the early lead miners who lived underground and bore this nickname. Wisconsin is also known as the *Copper State* in honor of its copper mines.

State Flower

The wood violet, *Viola papilionacea*, was adopted as the state flower in 1949. The flower had been selected in 1909 by schoolchildren.

State Tree

Wisconsin schoolchildren voted in 1948 and selected the sugar maple, *Acer saccharum*, as the state tree. That choice was made official in 1949.

State Bird

Wisconsin schoolchildren voted for the robin, *Turdus migratorius*, in 1926-27, but the state legislature did not make it official state bird until 1949.

State Animal

The badger, *Taxidea taxus*, was selected state animal in 1957.

State Domestic Animal

The dairy cow has been the state domestic animal since 1971.

State Fish

The muskellunge, *Esox masquinongy*, was named state fish in 1955.

State Insect

The honeybee, *Apis mellifera*, was adopted as state insect in 1977.

State Mineral

Galena, the chief ore of lead, was selected in 1971.

State Rock

Red granite was adopted as state rock in 1971.

State Soil

Antigo silt loam has been the state soil since 1983.

State Symbol of Peace

The mourning dove, *Zenaidura macroura*, was named in 1971.

State Wildlife Animal

In 1957, the white-tailed deer, *Odocoileus virginianus*, was adopted as the state wildlife animal.

State Song

Originally written as a football fight song in 1909, "On, Wisconsin!" with words by J.S. Hubbard and Charles D. Rosa and music by William T. Purdy, was named the state song in 1959, although the lyrics had to be changed.

Population

The population of Wisconsin in 1992 was 5,006,591, making it the 18th most populous state. There are 92.2 persons per square mile.

Industries

The principal industries of Wisconsin are trade, services, transportation, communications, and agriculture. The chief manufactured products are machinery, foods, fabricated metals, transportation equipment, and paper and wood products. Wisconsin leads the nation in the production of dairy products.

Agriculture

The chief crops of the state are corn, beans, beets, peas, hay, oats, cabbage, and cranberries, and the chief products are milk, butter, and cheese. Wisconsin is also a livestock state, and there are estimated to be some 4 million cattle, 1.2 million hogs and pigs, 105,000 sheep, and

Indians scale the rocks of Wisconsin Dells, one of the state's most scenic regions.

4.2 million chickens and turkeys on its farms. Maple, birch, oak, and evergreen trees are harvested. Crushed stone, sand, gravel, and lime are important mineral products. Commercial fishing earned $5.9 million in 1992.

Government

The governor of Wisconsin is elected for a four-year term, as are the lieutenant governor, secretary of state, attorney general, treasurer, and state superintendent of public instruction. The legislature consists of a 33-member senate and a 99-member assembly. Senators are elected from 33 senatorial districts and serve four-year terms. Assemblymen are elected from 99 assembly districts and serve two-year terms. The most recent state constitution was adopted in 1848. In addition to its two U.S. senators, Wisconsin has nine representatives in the U.S. House of Representatives. The state has 11 votes in the electoral college.

Sports

Wisconsin is a sports state. On the collegiate level, the University of Wisconsin has won the NCAA national hockey championship (1973, 1977, 1981, 1983, 1990) and the NCAA national basketball championship

(1941). Marquette University has won the NCAA national basketball championship (1977) and the National Invitation Tournament (1970).

On the professional level, the Milwaukee Brewers of the American League play baseball in Milwaukee County Stadium, and the Green Bay Packers of the National Football League play at Lambeau Field and County Stadium. The Milwaukee Bucks of the National Basketball Association play their games at the Bradley Center.

Major Cities

Green Bay (population 96,466). Settled in 1764, Green Bay is Wisconsin's second busiest port. The region was claimed for King Louis XII of France in 1634, and was named La Baye in 1669 when it became the site of a mission. It is the oldest settlement in the state.

Things to see in Green Bay: Heritage Hill State Park,

Beaupre Place (1840), Baird Law Office (1835), Roi-Porlier-Tank Cottage (1750), Fort Howard (1833-34), Neville Public Museum, National Railroad Museum, Hazelwood (1837-38), Green Bay Packer Hall of Fame, and Bay Beach Amusement Park and Wildlife Sanctuary.

Madison (population 190,766). Settled in 1837, Madison was a wilderness when the site was selected to be the capital of the territory in 1836. This "City of Four Lakes" is today a center of government and education. It has a rich architectural heritage left by Frank Lloyd Wright and the Prairie School movement.

Things to see in Madison: State Capitol, G. A. R. Memorial Hall Museum, State Historical Museum, Elvehjem Museum of Art, Madison Art Center, Henry Vilas Park Zoo, Olbrich Gardens, First Unitarian Church, Bradley House, Airplane House, Dr. Arnold Jackson House, Lamp House, J. C. Pew House, "Jacobs I" House, U.S.D.A. Forest

Products Laboratory, and Dane County Farmers' Market.

Milwaukee (population 628,088). Settled in 1822, Wisconsin's largest city was incorporated as a city in 1846. It was called *Millioki* by the Indians, which meant "gathering place by the waters." Today, "the machine shop of America" is one of the nation's top industrial cities.

Things to see in Milwaukee: War Memorial Center, Milwaukee Art Museum, Villa Terrace, Charles Allis Art Museum, Bradford Beach, City Hall (1895), Pabst Theater (1895), Milwaukee County Historical Center, Old World Third Street, Milwaukee Public Museum, Court of Honor, Northwestern Coffee Mills, St. Joan of Arc Chapel, Haggerty Museum of Art, Captain Frederick Pabst Mansion (1893), Milwaukee County Zoo, Mitchell Park Horticultural Conservatory, Annunciation Greek Orthodox Church, Lowell Damon House (1844), Kilbourntown House (1844), Schlitz Audubon Center, and Whitnall Park.

The exhibits at the Milwaukee Public Museum reflect the natural and human history of the state.

Places to Visit

The National Park Service maintains five areas in the state of Wisconsin: Apostle Islands National Lakeshore, Ice Age National Scientific Reserve, St. Croix National Scenic Riverway, Chequamegon National Forest, and Nicolet National Forest. In addition, there are 54 state recreation areas.

Baileys Harbor: Bjorklunden. A replica of a Norwegian chapel, or *stavkirke*, is located on this 325-acre estate.

Baraboo: Circus World Museum. This museum displays equipment used by the Ringling brothers' circus, which started here in 1884.

Belmont: First Capitol State Park. The 1836 council house and supreme court building have been restored.

Downsville: Caddie Woodlawn Country Park. Two 100-year-old houses and a log smokehouse are located in this memorial to the pioneer girl made famous in *Caddie Woodlawn* and *Magical Melons.*

Eagle: Old World Wisconsin. An outdoor museum recreates the pioneer life of German, Norwegian, Danish, and Finnish farmers.

Eagle River: Trees for Tomorrow Natural Resources Education Center. Demonstration forests and nature trails are part of this environmental education development.

Eau Claire: Paul Bunyan Logging Camp. This is a restored 40-man logging camp, with several 19th-century buildings.

Egg Harbor: Chief Oshkosh Indian Museum. This museum contains the possessions of the Menominee Indian chief and other Indian artifacts.

Ephraim: Pioneer Schoolhouse Museum. A restored schoolhouse (1869) and log cabin (1857) are among the exhibits.

Manitowoc: Maritime Museum. The World War II submarine USS *Cobia* can be toured.

Mineral Point: Pendarvis, Cornish Restoration. Six restored log and limestone homes built by English miners in the 1840s are located here.

Minocqua: Jim Peck's Wildwood. This 30-acre park houses hundreds of animals native to the area.

Mount Horeb: Little Norway. A small Norwegian farmstead, including a wooden church, or *stavkirke,* dates back to 1856.

New Glarus: Swiss Historical Village. Replicas of the first buildings erected by settlers in the 1840s can be seen here.

Port Washington: Lizard Mound. Thirty-one examples of effigy mounds built by prehistoric Wisconsin Indians.

Prairie du Chien: Fort Crawford Medical Museum. Relics of 19th-century medicine are on display.

Rhinelander: Rhinelander Logging Museum. Exhibits describing the logging history of the area.

Richland Center: Eagle Cave. This large onyx cavern has stalactites, stalagmites, and fossils.

Spring Green: Taliesin Fellowship Buildings. This was the 200-acre estate of the architect Frank Lloyd Wright.

Washington Island: Rock Island State Park. Icelandic-style architecture and the Potawatomi Lighthouse (1836) can be seen here.

Watertown: Octagon House and First Kindergarten in the U.S.A. The house, built in 1854, contains a hanging staircase. The kindergarten, which began in 1856, was housed separately.

Waupaca: Doll Shop Museum. More than 3,500 antique and modern dolls and a large teddy bear display may be seen here.

Wisconsin Dells: Wisconsin Dells State Recreation Area. The Wisconsin River cut a seven-mile channel through soft sandstone, forming tall cliffs and strange rock formations, which can be seen on guided tours by boat.

Deer and other wildlife roam Jim Peck's Wildwood, a 30-acre park in Minocqua.

Events

There are many events and organizations that schedule activities of various kinds in the state of Wisconsin. Here are some of them.

Sports: Bay Days Festival (Ashland), Sno-Escapades (Bayfield), Musky Jamboree (Boulder Junction), American Birkebeiner (Cable), World Championship Snowmobile Derby (Eagle River), Chicago Historic Races' International Challenge (Elkhart Lake), Road America (Elkhart Lake), Walleye Weekend Festival and National Walleye Tournament (Fond du Lac), International Aerobatic

Championship (Fond du Lac), Lumberjack World Championships (Hayward), Paddle and Portage Canoe Race (Madison), World Championship Musky Classic (Manitowish Waters), Salmon-A-Rama (Racine), Great Wisconsin Dells Balloon Rally (Wisconsin Dells).

Arts and Crafts: Cherry and Apple Blossom Time (Baileys Harbor), Art Fair on the Square (Madison), E. K. Petrie's Indian Artifact and Antique Show and Sale (Oshkosh), Outdoor Arts Festival (Sheboygan).

Music: Wisconsin Opry (Baraboo), Dixieland Jazz Festival (Eau Claire), Birch Creek Music Center (Egg Harbor), Madison Symphony (Madison), Concerts on the Square (Madison), Marquette Hall's 48-Bell Carillon (Milwaukee), Milwaukee Ballet (Milwaukee), Florentine Opera of Milwaukee (Milwaukee), Skylight Opera Theatre (Milwaukee), Milwaukee Symphony (Milwaukee).

Entertainment: Wisconsin State Maple Syrup Festival and Pancake Day (Antigo), Croatian Day (Ashland), Apple Festival (Bayfield), Beaverfest (Beaver Dam), Winnebago Indian Pow-Wow (Black River Falls), Winter Festival (Cedarburg), Northern Wisconsin State Fair (Chippewa

The Milwaukee Summerfest celebrates summer every year with carnival rides, food and games.

Falls), Old Ellison Bay Days (Ellison Bay), Fyr-Bal Fest (Ephraim), Wisconsin Folk Festival (Fond du Lac), Waterfest (Oshkosh), EAA International Fly-In Convention (Oshkosh), Butter Festival (Reedsburg), Aquafest (Rice Lake), Richland Centerfest (Richland Center), Wannigan Days (St. Croix Falls), Holland Festival (Sheboygan), Sister Bay Fall Festival (Sister Bay), Head-of-the-Lakes Fair (Superior).

Tours: Stone and Century House Tour (Cedarburg), Fall Flyway Tours (Fond du Lac),

House and Garden Walk (Sturgeon Bay).

Theater: Cloak Theater (Appleton), Alpine Valley Music Theater (Elkhorn), Peninsula Players (Fish Creek), Theatre on the Bay (Marinette), Mabel Tainter Chautauqua of the Pinery (Menominee), Pabst Theater (Milwaukee), Performing Arts Center (Milwaukee), Northern Lights Summer Playhouse (Minocqua), *Song of Norway* (Mount Horeb), Wisconsin Shakespeare Festival (Platteville), American Players Theatre (Spring Green).

The terrain of Wisconsin is quite varied. Here, at Cave Point in Door County, rocky cliffs and trees create a scene distinctly different from other parts of the state.

Summer at one of Wisconsin's more than 8,500 lakes.

Big Manitou Falls create a majestic scene in their natural setting.

Above left:
Some of the state's more heavily wooded areas can be found in northern Wisconsin.

The Land and the Climate

Wisconsin's natural features include several important rivers, more than 8,500 lakes—including two of the Great Lakes, Michigan and Superior—low wooded hills, and a vast expanse of rolling plain. Most of the state was affected by a series of glaciers that began their onslaught about a million years ago. They leveled hilltops, filled in valleys, and formed the numerous lakes. The state has five land regions.

The Lake Superior Lowland is a flat plain that forms a narrow strip along the northern border of Wisconsin. The Superior Upland covers most of northern Wisconsin. It slopes gradually to the south and contains heavily forested hills and hundreds of small lakes. Tim's Hill in Price County, at 1,953 feet Wisconsin's highest point, is located here.

The Central Plain curves around the central part of the state. The eastern and northwestern parts of this region were glaciated, but the southern portion was little affected by the Ice Age. It is in the southern part that the Wisconsin River has carved out the breathtaking gorges of the Wisconsin Dells.

From the early history of the Winnebago, Dakota, and Menominee Indians to the present day, people have appreciated the pristine beauty of Wisconsin's more than 8,500 lakes, its wildlife, and its expanses of gently rolling plains and low wooded hills.

The Western Upland stretches along the western border from the south to about two-thirds of the way to the northern border. Here are found steep slopes and winding ridges that were untouched by the glaciers. Along the Mississippi River are some of the most awe-inspiring limestone and sandstone bluffs in the country.

The Great Lakes Plains extend from the Green Bay area to Illinois on the eastern edge of the state. The region is the richest agricultural section of Wisconsin.

Wisconsin's largest river is the Mississippi. Into it flow the Wisconsin River, whose channel is near the Fox River that flows to Lake Michigan. Other important rivers are the St. Croix, the Chippewa, and the Black, all of which, flow into the Mississippi. Lake Winnebago, the largest lake in the state, is 29 miles long, and is connected to the Fox River.

Wisconsin's continental, or mid-American, climate is subject to extremes of heat and cold. In the north, winters are likely to be severe, with heavy snowfall and low temperatures. In the southern part, particularly along Lake Michigan, the climate is milder. Rain averages between 28 and 32 inches annually, although snowfall ranges from 30 inches in the extreme southern portions to 100 inches or more along the steep northwestern slopes. Average temperatures range from 20 degrees F. in January to 68 degrees F. in July.

The History

When the first white settlers arrived in the early 1600s, they found Winnebago, Dakota, and Menominee Indians in what was to become the state of Wisconsin. These Indians lived in lodges made of bark, saplings, and rushes; they fished and hunted, and grew corn, beans, and squash as well. Other Indians who had been driven west by the white man began to move into the region—Chippewa, Sauk, Fox, Ottawa, Kickapoo, Huron, Miami, Illinois, and Potawatomi. These were eastern woodsmen whose way of life was similar to that of the local tribes.

The first white man to enter the area was the French explorer Jean Nicolet. This was in 1634, when he was looking for a Northwest Passage to the Far East; Nicolet landed on the shore of Green Bay, expecting to be greeted by Chinese officials. He was disappointed to meet Winnebago Indians and went back to Quebec to report that America was far larger than anyone had thought. About 20 years later, Pierre Esprit Radisson and Médart Chouart, Sieur de Groseilliers, explored the region while searching for furs. Father René Ménard, the first missionary to the Wisconsin Indians, arrived about 1660,

The Winnebago Indians were among the first known inhabitants of what is now Wisconsin. Here, present-day Winnebagos keep their traditions alive.

An engraving showing Union soldiers marching down a main street in Fond Du Lac, Wisconsin in 1861, the year in which the Civil War began.

and established a mission near what is now Ashland. Other French missionaries and explorers followed, and France began to become interested in the area. The first French fort was built near Prairie du Chien in 1686, at the point where the Wisconsin joins the Mississippi.

The fur trade was to go on for over 150 years, with the French naming places and features of the land: La Crosse, Eau Claire, Fond du Lac, Butte des Morts, Flambeau, Lac Vieux Desert. But as late as 1820, there were only two settlements in the state—Green Bay and Prairie du Chien—each with about 500 people.

After the French and Indian Wars, Wisconsin had passed to the control of the British (1763), and English fur traders moved in when the region became part of the Province of Quebec. After the Revolution, of course, Wisconsin was American territory. First it was a section of the Indiana Territory, from 1800 to 1809; for 10 years after that it belonged to the Illinois Territory, after which it became part of the Michigan Territory, from 1818 to 1836. During the 1820s lead deposits were found in the southwest region, and miners poured into the area, some of them living in caves they had dug in the hillsides.

These cavemen were called "Badgers," for the ground-dwelling animal that is famous for its digging abilities. It became the nickname for Wisconsonites.

After the Black Hawk War of 1832, most of the native Indians had been driven out of Wisconsin: in 1836 Congress created the Wisconsin Territory. The territorial legislature met first in Belmont, later in Burlington (now a part of Iowa), and finally in Madison, which became the capital of the territory and later of the state. Wisconsin joined the Union as the 30th state in 1848, and Nelson Dewey was elected the first governor.

Newcomers began pouring into the state—miners from Cornwall in England, Yankee farmers, Irish, Norwegians, Germans, and Swiss. In the early 1900s, more people came from Poland, Holland, Belgium, Denmark, Iceland, and other countries. They were attracted by the availability of land and the state's many natural resources, including good soil and water, minerals, great forests, and abundant vegetation and game.

During the Civil War, Wisconsin generals at various times commanded the Iron Brigade, one of the Union's outstanding fighting groups, most of whose members were from Wisconsin. In the early 1900s, under the leadership of Governor Robert M. LaFollette, Sr., a member of the Progressive Party, Wisconsin established many forward-looking policies. Among them were regulation of railroad rates and services, a direct primary law, a labor-relations board, a teachers' pension plan, a workman's compensation law, minimum-wage laws, and pensions for mothers.

In 1950, Wisconsin Republican senator Joseph McCarthy began a crusade against those he called known communists and state employees he accused of internal subversion. His actions were later condemned by a senate vote of 67-22, but not before many careers and lives were ruined by his interrogations. More recently, Wisconsin's progressive social legislation has resulted in the first state gay rights legislation passed in 1982. In 1983, the Milwaukee school board filed charges against state and suburban school boards claiming that they

Milwaukee, Wisconsin's largest city, is an important center for industry and manufacturing.

Little Norway, located in Mount Horeb, represents the Norwegian influences that have helped to shape Wisconsin's identity.

Traditional costumes and dances are key elements in this Lithuanian Folk Fair.

interfered with the integration of suburban schools.

During World War II, Wisconsonites distinguished themselves for their contribution to the war effort. The products and produce of their factories and farms were valuable assets to the nation. Today, the state remains the nation's leading producer of dairy products and a major source of poultry, beef, potatoes, forest products, and grain crops. The great manufacturing centers of Milwaukee, Racine, Kenosha, Madison, and Green Bay produce, heavy machinery, processed foods, paper, and transportation equipment.

Education

Wisconsin is a state of education firsts. The first U.S. kindergarten was established in Waterton by Mrs. Carl Schurz in 1865. The first

Wisconsin public elementary school was founded in 1845 by Michael Frank in Kenosha, followed by the first Wisconsin public high school four years later. The state-supported University of Wisconsin has 12 campuses throughout Wisconsin.

The People

About two-thirds of the citizens of Wisconsin live in cities, almost one-third of them in the Milwaukee Metropolitan Area. About 96 percent of the people were born in the United States. Most of those who were born in foreign countries came from Germany, Norway, Poland, Russia, and Yugoslavia. Church membership in the state is about evenly divided between the Roman Catholic and the various Protestant churches.

A Winnebago youngster in his traditional headdress and shirt.

Frank Lloyd Wright, perhaps the greatest architect of modern times and a native of Wisconsin, built his famous house, *Taliesin*, on this site in Spring Green. It is now the home of Taliesin Associates, a school of architecture dedicated to carrying on Wright's work.

Famous People

Many famous people were born in the state of Wisconsin. Here are a few:

John Bardeen 1908-1991, Madison. Two-time Nobel Prize-winning physicist

Carrie Chapman Catt 1859-1947, Ripon. Women's rights leader

Zona Gale 1874-1938, Portage. Author

Hamlin Garland 1860-1940, West Salem. Author; one of the early Realists of American Literature

Herbert S. Gasser 1888-1963, Platteville. Noble Prize-winning physiologist

Arnold L. Gesell 1880-1961, Alma. Child psychologist

King C. Gillette 1855-1932, Fond du Lac. Safety razor manufacturer

Eric Heiden b. 1958, Madison. Olympic gold medal-winning speed skater

The magician and escape artist Harry Houdini spent his life getting out of ropes, shackles, and various locked containers.

Harry Houdini 1874-1926, Appleton. Magician

Vinnie Ream Hoxie 1847-1914, Madison. Sculptor

Curly Lambeau 1898-1965, Green Bay. Hall of Fame football coach

Robert Marion LaFollette 1855-1925, Primrose. Political leader

Liberace 1919-1987, West Allis. Pianist

Alfred Lunt 1893-1977, Milwaukee. Stage actor

Fredric March 1897-1975, Racine. Academy Award-winning actor: *Dr. Jekyll and Mr. Hyde*

Joseph R. McCarthy 1908-57, Grand Chute. Senator who lead a special senate subcommittee on internal subversion

Georgia O'Keeffe 1887-1986, Sun Prairie. Painter

William Rehnquist b. 1924, Milwaukee. Supreme Court Chief Justice

John Ringling 1866-1936, near Baraboo. Circus owner

Al Simmons 1902-1956, Milwaukee. Hall of Fame baseball player

Red Smith 1905-1982, Green Bay. Sports writer

Spencer Tracy 1900-1967, Milwaukee. Academy Award-winning actor: *Boys Town, Guess Who's Coming to Dinner*

Orson Welles 1915-1985, Kenosha. Academy Award-winning actor and director: *Citizen Kane*

Gene Wilder b. 1935, Milwaukee. Film actor: *The Producers, Young Frankenstein*

Laura Ingalls Wilder 1867-1957, Pepin. Novelist: *Little House on the Prairie, On the Banks of Plum Creek*

Thornton Wilder 1897-1975, Madison. Three-time Pulitzer Prize-winning novelist and playwright: *The Bridge of San Luis Rey, Our Town*

Frank Lloyd Wright 1869-1959, Richland Center. Architect

Colleges and Universities

There are many colleges and universities in Wisconsin. Here are the more prominent, with their locations, dates of founding, and enrollments.

Alverno College, Milwaukee, 1887, 2,514

Beloit College, Beloit, 1846, 1,187

Cardinal Stritch College, Milwaukee, 1937, 5,150

Carroll College, Waukesha, 1846, 2,108

Carthage College, Kenosha, 1847, 2,092

Edgewood College, Madison, 1927, 1,692

Lakeland College, Sheboygan, 1862, 2,656

Lawrence University, Appleton, 1847, 1,202

Marian College of Fond du Lac, Fond du Lac, 1936, 2,271

Marquette University, Milwaukee, 1881, 11,017

Mount Mary College, Milwaukee, 1913, 1,526

Ripon College, Ripon, 1851, 793

St. Norbert College, De Pere, 1898, 1,981

University of Wisconsin—Eau Claire, 1916, 10,431; *Green Bay,* 1968, 4,801; *La Crosse,* 1909, 8,362; *Madison,* 1848, 43,196; *Menomonie,* 1891, 7,343; *Milwaukee,* 1956, 24,341; *Oshkosh,* 1871, 11,039; *Platteville,* 1866, 5,225; *River Falls,* 1874, 5,440; *Stevens Point,* 1894, 8,545; *Superior,* 1893, 2,891; *Whitewater,* 1868, 10,512

Viterbo College, La Crosse, 1890, 1,392

Where To Get More Information

Wisconsin Dept. of Development Division of Tourism 123 W. Washington Ave. Madison, WI 53702 or call, 800-372-2737

Further Reading

General

Aylesworth, Thomas G., and Virginia L. Aylesworth. *Stat Reports: The Western Great Lakes: Illinois, Iowa, Minnesota, Wisconsin.* New York: Chelsea House, 1992.

Illinois

Bridges, Roger D., and Rodney O. Davis. *Illinois, Its History and Legacy.* St. Louis: River City Publishers, 1984.

Fradin, Dennis B. *From Sea to Shining Sea: Illinois.* Chicago: Childrens Press, 1991.

Lathrop, Ann, and others. *Illinois: Its People and Culture,* Minneapolis: Denison, 1975

Jensen, Richard J. *Illinois: A Bicentennial History.* New York: Norton, 1978.

Nelson, Ronald E., ed. *Illinois: Land and Life in the Prairie State.* Dubuque: Kendall/Hunt, 1978.

Stein, R. Conrad. *America the Beautiful: Illinois.* Chicago: Childrens Press, 1987.

Iowa

Fradin, Dennis B. *From Sea to Shining Sea: Iowa.* Chicago: Childrens Press, 1993.

Kent, Deborah. *America the Beautiful: Iowa.* Chicago: Childrens Press, 1991.

Posten, Margaret L. *This Is the Place—Iowa,* 3rd ed. Ames: Iowa State University Press, 1971.

Wall, Joseph F. *Iowa: A Bicentennial History.* New York: Norton, 1978.

Minnesota

Aylesworth, Thomas G., and Virginia L. Aylesworth, *Minnesota.* Greenwich, CT: Bison Books, 1986.

Blegen, Theodore C. *Minnesota: A History of the State,* 2nd ed. Minneapolis: University of Minnesota Press, 1975.

Lass, William E. *Minnesota: A Bicentennial History.* New York: Norton, 1977.

Lass, William E. *Minnesota, A History.* New York: Norton, 1983.

Rosenfelt, Willard E. *Minnesota: Its People and Culture.* Minneapolis: Denison, 1973.

Stein, R. Conrad. *America the Beautiful: Minnesota.* Chicago: Childrens Press, 1991.

Wisconsin

Austin, H. Russell. *The Wisconsin Story: The Building of a Vanguard State,* 3rd. ed. Milwaukee: Milwaukee Journal, 1964.

Carpenter, Allan. *Wisconsin,* rev. ed. Chicago: Childrens Press, 1978.

Dean, Jill W., ed. *Wisconsin,* Middleton: Tamarack Press, 1978.

Isherwood, Justin. *Wisconsin.* Portland: Graphic Arts Center, 1981.

Paul, Justus F. and B. D., eds. *The Badger State: A Documentary History of Wisconsin.* Grand Rapids: Eerdman's, 1979.

Stein, R. Conrad. *America the Beautiful: Wisconsin.* Chicago: Childrens Press, 1987.

Numbers in italics refer to illustrations

McCormick, Cyrus H., 21
Madison (WI), *73*, 76, 78, 90
Marquette, Jacques, 19, 43
Menominee Indians, 87
Michigamea Indians, 19
Milwaukee (WI), 78, *81*, 89, *89*, 90, 91
Minneapolis (MN), 56, *56*, 65
Minnesota, 49-70; area, 51; capital, *51*, 54;
   climate, 61; government, 55; map, 50;
   places to visit, 56-58; population, 51, 54;
   state bird, *51*, 54; state drink, 54; state
   fish, 54; state flag, *51*, 53; state flower,
   51, 54; state gem, 54; state grain, 54;
   state motto, 53; state mushroom, 54;
   state name, 54; state seal, 49, *49*; state
   song, 54; state tree, 54; as territory, 66
Mississippi River, 16, 17, 18, 24, 39, 42, 43,
   65, 86, 88
Missouri River, 39, 42
Moingwena Indians, 19
Mound Builder Indians, 19, 43

N
Nicolet, Jean, 87
Nordic Festival, *67*

North West Company, 65
Northwest Passage, 87
Northwest Territory, 20

O
Ohio River, 16

P
Peoria Indians, 19
Potawatomi Indians, 20, 87
Prairie du Chien (WI), 88

R
Racine (WI), 90
Radisson, Pierre Esprit, 65, 87
Railroads, 21, 66, 89
Revolutionary War, 19, 66, 88
Rockford (IL), 12

S
St. Paul (MN), *51*, 54, 56, *59*, *65*
Sandburg, Carl, 23, 27
Sauk Indians, 19, 20-21, 44, 87
Shawnee Hills (IL), 17

Sibley, Henry H., 66
Sioux City (IA), 36
Sioux Indians, 43, 45, 65, 66, *66*
Springfield (IL), *6-7*, 10, 12, *13*, *15*, 21

W
War of 1812, 20, 66
Winnebago Indians, 19, 87, *87*, 91
Wisconsin, 71-93; area, 73; capital, *73*, 76;
   climate, 86; government, 77; map, *72*;
   places to visit, 79-80; population, 73, 77;
   state animal, 76; state bird, *73*, 76; state
   domestic animal, 76; state fish, 76; state
   flag, *73*; state flower, *73*, 76; state insect,
   76; state mineral, 76; state motto, 75;
   state name, 76; state rock, 76; state seal,
   71, *71*; state soil, 76; state song, 76; state
   symbol of peace, 76; state tree, 76; state
   wildlife animal, 76; as territory, 88-89
Wisconsin River, 83, 86, 88
World War I, 23, 45, 66
World War II, 24, 45, 90
Wright, Frank Lloyd, 23, 75, 78, 91

Photo Credits

Courtesy Illinois Department of Commerce and Community Affairs: pp. 5, 6, 7, 8-9, 14, 15; Courtesy Illinois Department of Commerce and Community Affairs, Terry Farmer, photographer: pp. 3 (top), 16, 17, 18; Courtesy the Iowa Department of Economic Development: pp. 3 (bottom), 31, 32-33, 35, 36, 37, 38, 39, 40-41, 42, 43, 45; Courtesy Iowa Governor's Office and the Iowa State Printing Office: p. 29; Courtesy of Macmillan Publishing Company: p. 69; Courtesy Minnesota Office of Tourism: pp. 4 (top), 51, 52-53, 55, 56, 57, 59, 60, 61, 62-63, 64, 66, 67, 68; Courtesy of Minnesota Secretary of State: p. 49; Courtesy National Portrait Gallery, Smithsonian Institution: pp. 22, 24; Courtesy New York Public Library/Stokes Collection: 20, 21, 65, 88; Courtesy of the State Historical Society of Wisconsin: p. 92; Courtesy Wisconsin Division of Tourism: pp. 4 (bottom), 73, 74-75, 77, 79, 80, 81, 82, 83, 84-85, 86, 87, 89, 90, 91; Courtesy of Wisconsin Secretary of State: p. 71; Courtesy of UPI: p. 47.

Cover photos courtesy of Illinois Department of Commerce and Community Affairs, Terry Farmer, photographer; the Iowa Department of Economic Development; Minnesota Office of Tourism; and Wisconsin Division of Tourism.